CW00392000

The
Wiccan
Handbook

a modern guide to the symbols,
spells and rituals of witchcraft

Susan Bowes

An Hachette UK Company
www.hachette.co.uk

First published in 2003 by Godsfield Press,
an imprint of Octopus Publishing Group Ltd
Carmelite House
50 Victoria Embankment
London, EC4Y 0DZ
www.octopusbooks.co.uk

This edition published 2021 by Pyramid.

ISBN: 978-0-7537-3461-2

A CIP catalogue record for this book is available from the British Library

Printed and bound in China

10 9 8 7 6 5 4 3 2

Publisher: Lucy Pessell
Designer: Hannah Coughlin
Editor: Sarah Kennedy
Editorial Assistant: Emily Martin
Production Controllers: Lucy Carter and Nic Jones
Illustrations: Itskatjas/Dreamstime.com

Contents

Introduction

Welcome to *The Wiccan Handbook* – a book on everything you need to know about witchcraft and wicca, designed to penetrate the mystique of magic so that you can use it to enhance your life.

Casting spells and conducting rituals helps us to access and activate a natural source of power that lies hidden within each and every one of us. Reading this book will help you break through the barrier of prejudice and fear that surrounds the work of witches, so that you can open the door to this world of miraculous happenings in complete safety.

Magic can bring you love, protect you from harm, help with healing, guard your home and family, and even boost your bank balance. It works in so many wonderful ways – provided that your intention is pure and your wish is to do good selflessly. But, if it's curses or hexes you're after, or anything else associated with the so-called black arts or devil-worship ("Double, double, toil and trouble"), you are in for a big disappointment. *The Wiccan Handbook* is only for students and practitioners of pristine white magic, and its key words are *to help* and *to heal*. Never *to hurt* or *to harm*. As long as you adhere to the sacred law of magic-making which is never to manipulate another person against their will, you cannot go wrong.

But before I go any further, let me confirm what you have probably already guessed: I am a thoroughly cosmopolitan white witch, "outing" alongside thousands of other witches in Britain who practice the old crafts in one way or another. More to the point, I am an armchair witch, and by that I mean that I do not belong to a coven. I am also without a familiar, because I have never found a cat, dog, or budgie that really can change into another shape, and my broomstick sits inert in the corner of my kitchen. And, for reasons that will become clear a little later on, I wouldn't be seen dead in a pointed hat.

Having said that, there are certain characteristics that most witches have in common. We adore thunder and lightning, spend hours hugging trees and talking to flowers and plants, take ages collecting special stones and sticks, and, of course, visiting sacred sites. Tarot cards, wind chimes, and crystal balls are every witch's best friends.

People like to put labels on things, so I suppose I am what is known as a pagan. The word 'pagan' derives from the Latin word *paganus* meaning a villager or rustic dweller. The word was used as an insult by the Roman military to anyone who was a civilian or an incompetent soldier. The Christians then adopted it, to hurl as a term of abuse at anyone who wasn't one of them. So much for their Christianity.

Magic can bring you love, protect you from harm, help with healing, guard your home and family and open your eyes to the beauty that surrounds us

After many, many years of looking into all manner of religions and spiritual beliefs, I am content with my own spiritual practice, which has no other aims than to live in harmony with nature, learn to accept and love myself and others unconditionally, and to release my fear of death, so that when the time comes, I greet it with joy rather than dread.

Unlike many high priestesses and some high priests, I do not believe I am the reincarnation of Cleopatra, or the wife of Tutankhamun, but I do believe that each and every one of us is here for a special karmic purpose – principally for our souls to grow and develop in light and love. And I'm sure I must have been on this Earth before, although, having said that, it's the here and now that matters.

I am a part of a profession that is much maligned and misunderstood – thanks to the "witchy" images of cobwebs, sorcery, and elemental superstition, which are, plain and simple, a hangover from medieval days. However, it is a profession that continues to fascinate people and one that has refused to lie down and die. Its power is ever-present in our modern society, as can be seen from the increase in spiritual practices all over the world.

Despite this, the notion of the witch, the wand, and the magical spell still calls to the child within every adult, just as it did when we sat entranced at the pantomime or enthralled by the bedtime story. The young mind is open to worlds where everything is possible, before adult rationalism curtails our imagination. But part of us wants to believe in the impossible. Judging by the ever-increasing popularity of science-fiction books and films, this thirst is unquenchable.

The Wiccan Handbook offers a way of rekindling the old magic for yourself, away from television programmes and videos, taking you right back to the very heart of nature. Without nature there is no magic. This is a book of simple, yet highly effective, keys and codes, of incantations, cosmic recipes, and beautiful ancient symbolism; a sort of language to help you reach through the veil into this unseen world.

Sadly, the word "witchcraft" connotes so many negative ideas and opinions that it is important to demystify its meaning before we go on. The word "witchcraft" is derived from the old Celtic word *wicca* (or the feminine *wicce*), meaning "wise." Those who practiced the ancient wicca crafts could actually "bend" reality and therefore appear to create magic. The word "magic" comes from the ancient Middle Eastern word *magi*, the literal translation of which is "wise men" or priests (as in "We Three Kings of Orient Are"). The more modern interpretation of magic given by the dictionary is "seeking to harness and conduct psychic forces to cause manifestation by using appropriate incantations, spells, and charms to focus the mind!"

As I am sure you are well aware, the practice of witchcraft has landed its adepts in extremely hot water over the centuries, culminating in the terrifying persecution of witches throughout Europe in the Middle Ages. But why, when magic and forms of witchcraft have been interwoven into the fabric of our culture since time began?

The Practice of Black Magic

This world is very odd we see
We do not comprehend it
But in fact we all agree
God won't and we can't mend it.

Arthur Hugh Clough, 1819–1861

Before we go into the history of witchcraft and why it is shrouded in such negativity, here are a few words of warning about the practice of black magic.

As I have already emphasized, using any form of magic to hurt or harm another living creature has no place in witchcraft, and this includes the manipulation of another person against their will, casting hexes or curses, or controlling another through threat or fear. The law of the Universe is quite simple: cause chaos or harm to another being and it will rebound on the practitioner with ten times as much force.

Using any form of magic to hurt or harm another living creature has no place in witchcraft

It is very important to make this abundantly clear, because many people will automatically associate black magic with witchcraft, although this association is a legacy of the magnificently successful propaganda campaign that was waged by the Christian Church against innocent wise people who practiced the old crafts during medieval days.

Nevertheless, to say that the practice of black magic does not exist would be arrogantly naive. But its practitioners are meddling with forces far beyond their control, which can only lead their souls into the darkest hour.

Creating black magic is not witchcraft. Black magic does not follow the craft of the wise. Its rituals have no bearing on the work of the wicca or wicce practitioner, because no real witch would ever perform a ceremony to invoke harm on any level.

There is good and bad in every walk of life and the physical world gives us the opportunity to choose the direction in which we wish to express ourselves creatively. At any moment we can elect to change direction. But one thing is quite clear – a loving soul will sleep peacefully at night.

Part 1:

The Story of Witchcraft

The Early Times

Throughout the ancient world there is indisputable evidence that most religions were dedicated to goddess worship. It was the goddess who provided the nurturing and nourishment that man needed in order to survive. The priestess would act as her channel, and the priest – far from being an autocratic patriarchal figurehead – became her consort and conduit of power, so reflecting the natural male/female balance of nature. The priestess represented the feminine, dark mysteries of the moon, and the priest the masculine heat and fervor of the sun. This formed the root of all religions.

The word "religion" comes from the Latin word *religio* meaning conscientiousness and piety, from which comes the verb *religare*: to tie or to fasten, as in "ligament." Furthermore, the Latin word *religens* is affiliated to this root, meaning "fearing the gods." Note the plural!

From early times god and goddess magic was called upon to bless the fertility of the earth and the safety of farm crops and animals. Ritual dances were created to harness this energy, by leaping and jumping in the manner depicted in an ancient hymn dedicated to Zeus, which entreated him to leap for the well-being of the herds, crops, and communities of Crete. The word "leap" is a pun on sexually covering or

> From early times
> magic was called
> upon to bless the
> fertility of the earth
> and the safety of farm
> crops and animals

jumping a maiden, and sex magic has been used throughout the ages to ensure, among other things, fertility and prosperity for the coming year. Ancient kings of Mesopotamia, it is said, went through sacred marriages with the goddess Ishtar, who was represented by a priestess of high rank. Another ritualistic custom practised in the ancient world was circumcision, the ultimate offering to the goddess Isis. This act of sacrifice was linked to the legend of Isis and Osiris – a wonderful story steeped in mysterious symbolism which perhaps opens the door to understanding the powerful part that goddess energy has always played in witchcraft. We will explore this legend (see pages 22–3), but first we must look at why witchcraft needed to go underground in order to survive.

It all began to change with the birth of the Christian Church. Up until that time, the priestess played a leading role in religious worship. She was revered as the sacred representation of mother earth and sister moon, the provider, nurturer, and mystical teacher – Isis incarnate. Enter the destruction of the matriarchal religions, the disempowerment of women, and the onset of negative connotations of witchcraft.

Witchcraft has always been regarded as essentially feminine magic aligned with lunar energy, stemming from the days when it was a woman's work to grow and harvest plants and herbs, while the men did the more manual labor and hunted.

Women learned how the potency of plants responded to the phases of the moon, the time of day or night, and the seasons of the year. They also learned to create powerful and highly effective spells, perfumes, poisons, and potions to entice, destroy, manipulate, defeat, challenge, fascinate, and confuse. Or at least that is how the fragile male ego began to view it. Because she possessed enigmatic knowledge and abstruse healing powers, the witch that is women from rural areas in general began, over time, to be regarded as a threat to the very foundation of male dominance.

In 1258 Pope Alexander IV issued the first papal letter to empower the Inquisition to deal with witchcraft, but only when witchcraft was "manifestly savored on heresy." In doing so, he laid the basis for the persecution of any woman who dared step out of line, especially those who were healers or possessed scientific knowledge that might be regarded as a threat to male supremacy. The Church was pretty intolerant of females who educated themselves, thought for themselves, or embraced any other religious belief, such as paganism or witchcraft. In short, men were frightened of women's power.

Things began to get more uncomfortable in Europe during the 1400s when Pope Eugenius IV put yet more pressure on the Inquisition to root out magicians and fortune-tellers (or diviners, as they were called). Wild accusations of crones flying on broomsticks to attend the witches' synagogue (the name taken from the Jewish tradition as an insult to their customs – Jewish persecution being rife), where they

Witchcraft has always been regarded as essentially feminine magic aligned with lunar energy

were said to practice cannibalism and indulge in orgies and other unmentionable goings-on, fulled the fire of accusation and counter-accusation.

The Malleus Maleficarum, also known as *The Hammer of Witches*, was written by Jacob Sprenger and Heinrich Krämer, two ardent Dominican monks, and published in 1486, principally to counteract any skepticism about witchcraft. It laid down cruel and stringent regulations for the interrogation of suspects and for trials of the accused. Interestingly, it also recommended the use of "Christian Magic" to ward off bewitchment. This Christian magic, witchcraft in fact, included prayer, using the sign of the Cross for protection, and sprinkling the body with holy water, blessed by the priest, to which a pinch of rue, rosemary, and peony (all said to deter witches) had been added, together with some salt. Salt is a well-known scourge or cleanser for any form of negativity or psychic attack.

Matters really began to hot up around the 1520s, with the onset of witch-hunts, primarily in Italy. In 1523 it was reported that around one hundred witches a year were being burned in Como. There was then a lull for about thirty-five years, before the persecution began again, with ever greater rapaciousness. The reason, of course, was the creation of the Protestant Church by Henry VIII. Catholics were incensed by his audacity at placing himself at the head of his own Church. Men on both sides of the religious divide, being obsessed with power and control, accused each other of being the servants of the Devil, and witches quickly became the scapegoats. There followed what can only be described as mass genocide. In fact, such was the ferocity of the Catholic-led witch-hunts and the subsequent burnings at the stake, in parts of Germany, that it was stated at the time that hardly any old woman was safe. The children of the condemned were horrifically punished as well by being stripped and beaten round the fire that was burning their parent alive. This shameful campaign naturally targeted Protestants and Jews as well.

Contrary to popular belief, English witches did not suffer the same persecution as their Scottish or European counterparts, principally because the use of torture to obtain confessions of witchcraft was outlawed in England. Nor were they burned at the stake. Instead they were beaten up and hanged. The reason for this lay in the fact that, in Protestant England, witchcraft was associated with sorcery and was therefore regarded as a civil crime, while on the continent and in Scotland it was a crime of heresy against the Catholic Church.

Spotting a witch was an arbitrary task. Single women were at the greatest risk, possibly because they lived longer than men, and also because more of them survived the plague. What was their dastardly secret? In 1657 the Reverend John Gaule, vicar of Great Staughton, Hungerford, England, proclaimed:

"Every old woman with a wrinkled face, a furr'd brow, a hairy lip, a gobber tooth, a quint eye, a squeaking voice, or a scolding tongue having a rugged coat on her back, a skull cap on her head, a spindle in her hand, and a dog or cat by her side, is not only suspect but pronounced a witch."

Other signs to look out for in a suspected witch included her inability to cry, and faltering while saying the Lord's Prayer. If she weighed less than the church Bible (which, to be fair, was pretty hefty), then that was a sure sign of guilt. Any form of blemish, birthmark, wart, scar, cyst, or mole was considered the Devil's mark, and any unusual swellings or lumps provided indisputable evidence that the person in question was feeding a "familiar" – a familiar being a demon-helper that lived with the offender and could take on the shape of an animal, such as a black cat. To test the suspect, pins were stuck into her body. If no blood was drawn, this was a sure sign of devilry. Witches also had to go through a swimming ordeal. Bound hand and foot, they were thrown into the local river. If they floated or, as their accusers assumed, were held up by the Devil, they were guilty and were immediately dispatched to a horrible death. If they sank, they were innocent but also drowned!

It is estimated that around 1,000 people were executed for witchcraft in England over a period lasting one hundred years or so. Matthew Hopkins was the most notorious witch-hunter and scoured the land during the 1640s, hanging over sixty people in Essex alone in one year. Such was his persecution mania that public support finally turned against him and in 1647 he was tried by his own methods, thrown into the river,

and, on finding that he floated, was denounced as a wizard. The last three hangings of witches in England occurred in 1682 at Exeter, and the last woman to be tried for, and convicted of, witchcraft was Jane Wenham, from Hertfordshire, in 1712. She, fortunately, was reprieved. Scottish witches fared rather worse. Over 4,000 were executed mostly by burning at the stake, between 1590 and 1680. The last execution took place in 1727.

Witch-hunts in Ireland never really took hold, even though witchcraft had been practiced there since the twelfth century. This was principally because the Catholic and Protestant Churches were too busy fighting each other.

America did not escape the persecution, either. Immigrants from Europe imported their beliefs to the New World and, as a consequence, there were eleven hangings in Connecticut between 1647 and 1662. But the most famous witch-hunt occurred in Salem, Massachusetts, in 1692, when an adolescent girl began to suffer fits and other children became hysterical. This was immediately assumed to be the working of witchcraft. Nineteen men and women were hanged at the same time for "joining the Devil to destroy the Church of God." Another

> **Most of these victims of religious piety were simply misunderstood wise women, healers, herbalists, and midwives**

member of the group was pressed to death for refusing to plead. The atrocity did not go down well with the majority of the people and four years later the jurors of the trial signed a Confession of Error saying that they had been misled by the Devil!

All in all, it is thought that around one million witches were put to a terrible death throughout Europe during those dark years of persecution – the last being in France in 1745 and as late as 1775 in Germany. However, in her book *Woman, Church and State*, Matilda Gage claims that over nine million were slaughtered over a period of 300 years.

It is salutary to remember that most of these victims of religious piety were simply misunderstood wise women, healers, herbalists, and midwives, or were people of a different religious persuasion and those who owned their own properties, upon which the authorities cast a greedy eye.

The decline of witch-hunting came about not because witchcraft was stamped out, but because adverse public opinion made the "Establishment" reconsider its actions and finally turn against witch-hunts for fear of losing the support of the masses.

The Legend of Isis and Osiris

The greatest of all goddesses comes from Egyptian mythology… Isis, the embodiment of the female divinity. It is said that she was begat through an incestuous liaison between Nut, the goddess of the heavens and her erstwhile earth-god brother Geb. This union was severely frowned upon by Ra, the sun god, who commanded their father to part them. This he did, with Nut arching away from her brother to form the sky and Geb forming the earth. However Nut was pregnant. This angered Ra so much that he forbade her to give birth on any day of his year – which then consisted of 360 days. Poor Nut was doomed to perpetual pregnancy.

Until that is, Thoth, god of magic, the moon, and karmic justice, who also controlled the movement of the stars, took pity on Nut and won her five extra days, which were added to the existing 360, making a new annual cycle of 365 days. Nut promptly gave birth to four children: Set, Isis, Osiris, and Nephthys.

Some legends say that Isis and Osiris had an "encounter" in the womb which produced Horus, a powerful sky god and falcon god, to whom Nut gave birth after the other four. And so these became the five heavy gods created in the flesh who were to reshape the world.

Isis became queen to Osiris and during his absence she ruled supreme and grew to be loved and revered by all. But Set, their brother, grew increasingly jealous of Osiris's success and rather covetous of Isis, even though he was by then married to Nephthys. He decided to terminate Osiris. Set devised a dastardly plan and tricked Osiris into lying in an open coffin, the lid of which was quickly sealed and the whole thing thrown into the River Nile.

Isis was devastated and immediately set out in search of her husband, but Set outplayed her. Before she could find Osiris's body to restore it to life, Set had him chopped up into fifteen

And so these five became the heavy gods created in the flesh who were to reshape the world

pieces, the parts of which were scattered far and wide. Isis became demented in her search for Osiris's parts and, helped by Nephthys (who probably wanted to get her own back on her wayward husband), located fourteen of them. The fifteenth part, his penis, unfortunately remaining missing. But Thoth allowed Isis to conceive another child from the dead body of Osiris, by providing a wooden phallus. Some sources say that the child was Harpocrates, the god of secrecy and silence, while others say that this is really how Horus was begat.

Whatever the truth, Horus grew up quickly and unerringly pursued Set in order to reap revenge for his father's demise by castrating him. Isis became synonymous with the image of the devoted wife and mother, and was therefore adopted as the goddess of the moon and the emblem of the wise woman. The cow became her sacred emblem because it too nurtures and feeds mankind. The horns of the cow formed the base of her crown and represented the crescent moon, upon which sat the solar disc – symbol of the sun, thus combining the divine male and female principles.

An inscription is said to have been found on one of her statues stating:

I, Isis, am all that has been
That is or shall be
No mortal man hath ever me unveiled.

To lift the veil on Isis is to search into the great mysteries of life. Isis embodies many of the feminine principles, and because she lived as a woman among mankind, she became regarded as the great divine mother-goddess. Her unerring devotion to Osiris, and subsequent search for and burial of his body, so that he could attain rebirth and immortality, also won her great accolades among mortal man and the immortal gods. She was worshipped persistently up until as late as the sixth century a.d. at her own temple at Philae, near Aswan. The goddess Isis symbolizes all that is true and pure in woman, and this is why she plays such an important role in the life of witches.

The legend of Isis and Osiris became the cornerstone for other mythological legends, sagas, and tales, and to this day the gods have played a profound role in the evolution of our spiritual growth. While they themselves remain enigmas, their personalities and stories reflect the complexities of the human psyche, and the many challenges that the ego needs to overcome in order to progress from human to divine man.

In short, the myths of the gods were created as self-knowledge teaching stories, which opened up the path to oneness with the universal spirit. "New Age" thinking is a direct descendant. The goddess energy is a vital link between the unseen world and the world of the physical. Witches call on this energy in order to redress the balance of our patriarchally dominated society, and look to the goddess as their guide and mentor.

> **The legend of Isis and Osiris became the cornerstone for other mythological legends, sagas, and tales**

Modern Witchcraft

In the Western world, there is currently a massive revival in the practice of the old pagan religions, principally because of their close association with the healing power of nature.

Unlike their patriarchal religious counterparts, neither the

old nor the modern white witch would dream of attempting to cajole, coerce, or convert another against his or her will. Inherently respecting the choice of the individual, witches prefer to work quietly and privately, because they acknowledge and revere the wonders of life. As with any practice – religious or otherwise

> **Modern white witches are healers and protectors of the ancient secrets of nature**

– some witches are more ardent than others. Some are members of covens, who celebrate their religion on a regular yet informal basis, while others worship the goddess energy in temples and adhere to much stricter codes of rite, ritual, and ceremonial dress.

Modern white witches are, first and foremost, healers and protectors of the ancient secrets and old lores of nature. They celebrate the alchemical marriage of earth, air, fire, and water and use the magical and healing properties of herbs, plants, trees, crystals, colours, stones, and astrological energies to enhance and empower their work. But you don't have to go tramping the forests at night, take part in rituals on sabbats, join covens, attend high priestesses in temples, or don strange ceremonial garb to change your life! Magic can be performed most effectively, and quite safely, in the comfort of your own home just by learning a few golden rules and by understanding the basic laws of spell-casting.

The rest of this book will guide you step-by-step toward opening a door that will thrill and inspire you. I guarantee that your life will never be quite the same again.

Part 2:

Getting Started

The Tools of the Trade

First we need to take a look at the word "spell" in order to banish any preconceived notions that you may have about what the word means. According to its etymology, there are four definitions to be found.

The first is associated with the Gothic word *spill*, meaning a saying, story, narrative, or item of news. The word "gospel" comes from this – the literal translation being the narrative of God, or God's news. The second definition is the expression of words in letters of the alphabet – that is, to spell or write out. This is related to the Anglo-Saxon word *spellian*, meaning to recount. The third meaning is related to the old English word speld signifying a splinter or thin rod of wood, which was used to point out the spelling (as in teacher, rod, and blackboard). These thin rods were also called wands. The final definition of spell describes a period of work or activity.

To sum up, a spell is created by setting aside a period of time in which to recount something that spells out your desire, the energy of which is bound together and then focused by the wand. Hence the phrase "spellbinding" which is still used today.

You unwittingly create magic every day just through your thoughts. Magic is created simply by focusing thought – that is its secret

You will probably be astonished to learn that you unwittingly create magic every day just through your thoughts. Magic is created simply by focusing thought – that is its secret. The problem lies in the fact that most of us aren't clear enough about our lives to know what we want, or find that the pressure of everyday life prevents us from focusing our minds long enough to attain it.

That is why it is so important to set aside a sacred spell of time in which to create a special ceremony or ritual to draw in the energy so that you can really concentrate on what you desire. Once you have single-mindedly logged in your wish, the Universe has a chance to receive your message clearly and to manifest it for you. Just be open to receive.

At this point many people will throw up their hands in horror, saying I am promoting pure evil greed. My answer is that our personal lives are a direct reflection of our spiritual wealth, and someone who is spiritually wealthy never goes without. Thought is the most powerful tool available to us. If your life does not feed and nurture you, change your thought patterns and your life will automatically become brighter and lighter.

Magic-making is a delightful way of learning to take control of what you draw into your life and, indeed, what you banish from it. It is worth taking time to think about this before you begin to work with magic because it will change your life, often in the most unusual ways, and you need to be ready to let go of the old in order to let the new in.

The Altar

Spells go hand-in-hand with altars. This does not mean that you need to adjourn to the local church to commandeer its altar. Far from it. You can make your own special place on a table, windowsill, or, if you have one, on a mantelpiece – the fire beneath is a powerful symbol.

Most witches dedicate their altars to their personal goddess or god, and decorate it with precious crystals, talismans, herbs, flowers, and other ephemera. It is their focal point beside which they can sit quietly and meditate. Some witches place money on their altars, to be blessed by their deity, so that when they pass it on, the recipient also receives those blessings.

Altars should be placed facing north, because this is the realm of midnight and familiars, dreams, and magic: the direction from which power flows out of darkness into light.

> You can make your
> own special place on
> a table, windowsill,
> or, if you have
> one, on a mantelpiece

It is a well-known fact that we sleep better lying from north to south, and in churches, the Bible and the pulpit were often placed in the north because it was said that out of the darkness (from the north) comes the light (of the Word). Some witches, however, position their altars facing east to honour the rising of the sun.

I recommend that you use a special tablecloth to act as an altar cloth. Ritual work is sacred, and the items that you use should therefore be regarded in the same light.

Candles

Candles have been used as part of religious ceremonies – be they Christian, Jewish, Muslim, Hindu, or Buddhist – since the earliest times, principally because they represent the power of light (knowledge and spiritual illumination) coming out of the darkness (ignorance); the power of the angelic forces and the essence of the Ascended Masters. The ancient initiates used fire to symbolize the very spark of the divine life force that is within each and every one of us; it illumines the darkness of the soul, and leads it forwards on its path towards spiritual enlightenment. Witches also use candles to represent the element of fire, and, because candles create such a peaceful meditative ambience, they help to quieten the mind and to focus thought.

Candle magic is the most simple of rituals to perform. Take a few moments to centre yourself before lighting your candle; this marks the beginning of your ritual and signifies the call

Colour Codes

Colour plays an important role in magic-making, and witches generally have an array of coloured candles to use for different spells:

white: Purity, peace

red: Sexual energy, strength, courage

pink: Love, friendship

blue: Healing, truth, inspiration, higher wisdom

green: Abundance, fertility, good luck, harmony, money

yellow: Creative imagination, communication

purple: Spiritual power, psychic ability

orange/gold: Positive thinking, justice

silver: Channeling, clairvoyance, astral energies

to attendance of the angelic forces. Look into the flame and visualize your wish. Then blow out the candle as you release your wish. The smoke takes it up into the Universe.

Some witches score their candles with runic symbols or special patterns, although this is not essential. It is, however, important to use fresh candles which are not cracked or marked, for each spell. On no account should you relight ones used for decoration or as night-lights because they hold a different energy vibration from the ritual you are conducting, and the candles used in magic rituals need to burn down, even if it takes all night to do so. So make sure you always put your altar and candles in a safe place, where the candles cannot fall over and where it is away from drafts that might blow them out. Once alight, the candle should not be touched. Incidentally, candles should be lit with matches because they are made from the natural element of wood, rather than with a lighter, which contains petrol pollutant.

Oils

The art of making scented oils for healing and magical purposes dates back to well before the rise of the Egyptian dynasty. The concentrated essences of herbs and flowers are distilled into a carrier oil, which conserves the full aroma and vibration of the plant. Depending on the aroma, these perfumes stimulate the centres of the brain that control emotional, mental, and intellectual faculties, therefore effecting energetic changes in the body.

Throughout history, perfumes have also been worn to attract (or repel!) the opposite sex and to hide the odor of unwashed bodies. Oils were also used as a source of scented light, while sacred oils have been used in religious ceremonies since the earliest times as a means of sanctification and purification. In Exodus 30, God gives Moses clear instructions on how to blend a holy oil out of myrrh, cinnamon, calamus, and cassia in olive oil. "And thou shalt make it an oil of holy ointment, an ointment compound after the art of the apothecary; it shall be an holy anointing oil."

The three kings brought myrrh and frankincense to Jesus as

Oils

Every witch has a store of rosemary oil, which can be used for any type of spell-casting. Here is a list of other oils that resonate to specific desires.

love: Gardenia, jasmine, lavender, rose

lust: Basil, cinnamon, ginger, neroli, ylang ylang

prosperity: Almond, bergamot, honeysuckle, mint, peony

healing: Carnation, mimosa, rosemary, sandalwood

protection: Basil, frankincense, lavender, myrrh

luck: Allspice, nutmeg, orange, violet

business: Benzoin, cinnamon, mint, peony

money: Clove, ginger, honeysuckle, nutmeg, pine

success: Bergamot, clove, ginger, lemon balm

happiness: Lavender, lily of the valley, marjoram

sleep: Chamomile, lavender, peppermint, thyme

vitality: Bay, carnation, pennyroyal, St.-John's-wort

peace: Lavender, gardenia, passion flower, skullcap

blessings: Benzoin, cumin, rue

their offering of devotion, and ancient kings and queens were anointed with special oils at their death to preserve their bodies for the after-life. Indeed, they were buried with pots of oils and perfumes alongside precious gold and silver objects, which they would take with them to appease the gods.

The famous "flying ointment" said to be worn by witches to enable them to fly on their broomsticks at night was made from a blend of herbs and animal fat. In reality, the herbs contained hallucinogenic qualities, which opened the higher centres of consciousness, resulting in astral projection (rather than actual physical projection).

Oils still play an important part in magic ritual today because many witches anoint themselves to enhance their work. It is important to know that oil represents the element of fire, and by anointing a candle with oil, it acts as a message of intent as it burns with the candle. Use a combination of one, three, five, seven, or nine pure essential oils and drop them into a carrier oil such as grapeseed or almond, then rub them into the candle while concentrating on what you wish to manifest.

Essential oils are readily available at drugstores and pharmacies, although it is quite easy to make them yourself. Just cover the herb or flower with a carrier oil and put it into a tightly sealed bottle. Shake the bottle for a few minutes every day for a couple of weeks, then strain it through some cheesecloth, and you have your very own brew.

Herbs and Plants

The word "herb" comes from the old Sanskrit *bharb*, meaning to eat, which later became *herba* in Latin, meaning grass or fodder. Herbs are distinguishable from other plants and flowers because the stem does not become woody. Herbal magic, or wortcunning as it is known by country folk, is an essential part of magic-making, *wort* being the original Saxon word for herb, which has been preserved in names such as St.-John's-wort and figwort.

The use of the medicinal properties of herbs and plants is as old as time, and it is only in very recent centuries that scientists have turned their back on the natural healing resources that the Earth supplies to create debatable man-made curatives. Well-being is created by a healthy balance in mind, body, and spirit; one cannot be treated separately from another, and the gentle healing qualities of nature are specifically designed

to clear out our systems and perfectly re-balance our energy centres. Just looking up into a blue sky clears our minds because blue is the colour of healing and communication; a walk beside a vibrant yellow field of rape feeds our solar (sun-yellow) plexus area and helps our vital forces to flow.

Modern medicine has produced extraordinary miracles of its own, but it is a shame that alternative medicine is often viewed with skepticism by the medical profession. It is a documented fact that the ancient healers and mystics had to be adept in the sciences of astrology, astronomy, and herbal law if they were to study medicine. An holistic overview of mind, body, and spirit is now playing an increasingly important role in alternative diagnosis. A word of warning though – some plants are extremely poisonous, so unless you really know what you are doing, do not pick herbs and plants from the hedgerows. Always consult a qualified herbalist if you choose to pursue this path of healing.

Herbs

Here is a list of readily available herbs and plants that are affiliated to particular wishes and desires:

love: Apple, basil, dill, jasmine, lavender, thyme

wealth: Allspice, cedar, comfrey, ginger, honeysuckle

protection: Bay, clove, fennel, orris, pine, witch hazel

health: Cilantro, juniper, knotweed, nutmeg, oak, rue

fertility: Fig, geranium, mustard, patchouli, peach, poppy

courage: Black cohosh, borage, mullein, poke, yarrow

happiness: Catnip, celandine, hawthorn, hyacinth, marjoram

Plants, trees, shrubs, flowers, and herbs also embody different magical qualities, which resonate with the planetary forces in our solar system. These properties have also been used since time immemorial.

Perhaps the most famous of all the witches' herbs is mandrake. It is affiliated with the Egyptian god Thoth, and emanates powerful energies to attract protection, fertility, money, love, and health, apart from being a potent aphrodisiac. Its roots are said to suggest the appearance of a man, because, according to folklore, it grew from a dead man's seed, which fell as he was hanged for murder. People so revered the power of the mandrake that they would bury their entire savings near it, because they believed they would thereby increase!

If you are making your own blend of herbs to scatter on water or on the earth as a thanks offering to the goddess, make sure they are thoroughly dry, then place a few drops of essential oil with the mixture to create a pleasing perfume. If you are making incense, it is also advisable to include a resin such as myrrh or frankincense as a base to help it burn.

Incense

Incense is made by selecting and blending together certain herbs, spices, gums, resins, and oils, which, when burned, release an aroma that raises the vibration of the desired wish or notion. Because it acts on the olfactory organs, it also opens the higher centres of consciousness.

In ancient times incense was burned to evoke the gods and to purify the atmosphere during sacrifice. Later it was used to symbolize the sacrifice itself; the spiralling smoke carried messages up to the heavens. Incense was also used to purify bed-chambers and clothing, to protect homes and businesses, cure sickness, and deliver the soul of the departed into the hands of the gods. Incense-burning still plays an important religious role, particularly in Eastern religions.

All sorts of prepacked incenses, such as cones, sticks, and blocks, can be bought. I would suggest that you use incense that can be burned on a charcoal block, placed within a censer, or a dish robust enough to hold red-hot charcoal. Put a block of charcoal in your censer or heatproof dish, say your incantation, throw the incense onto the burning charcoal, and watch the smoke rise toward the heavens bearing your message.

Crystals and Stones

It is said that you don't choose crystals, they choose you. From my own experience, this would seem to be perfectly true, and when their time is done, they often "disappear" or you feel compelled to hand them onto someone else.

Crystals

This list is a guide to which colour of crystal to use in order to draw in the required energy:

white: Purifies the physical, emotional, and etheric bodies

pink: Represents love, self-respect, self-worth

red: Energy, sexual love

orange: Release from responsibility, creates a personal magnetic field

yellow: Mental awareness

green: Healing the heart, abundance, balance

turquoise: Intuition

blue: Healing, protection, strength

purple: Transformation, elevation of the soul

gold: Wisdom, self-confidence

brown: Stability and Earth

black: Material world, protection, absorption of negativity

Crystals are surely one of the most beautiful and magical gifts from the earth, and a wonderful complement to your altar and your magical work. Hold them in your hand while you are meditating, to help you focus on your intent, then either return them to the earth by burying them, or keep them in a safe place so they can transmute their energy.

Stones, too, have extraordinary powers, particularly stones with holes in them. These were traditionally called "hag stones," because it was said they acted as an amulet to protect the wearer against witches' spells! Country folk regarded them as harbingers of life, because the hole was a representation of feminine fertility and was therefore affiliated to the moon goddess Diana. Many witches collect twelve holy stones, together with a heart shaped stone which they arrange in a circle, with the heart stone marking the centre. This acts like a personal Stonehenge, empowering any object or spell placed within it.

Pen, Ink and Paper

To help manifest your dream, you need to write a list of your desires. You can of course use an ordinary ballpoint pen, but you may find using a special fountain or quill pen with some coloured inks helps to provide a sense of ceremony whilst channeling your deepest desires.

You may also need to draw a picture of what you desire, or make a collage or treasure map by cutting out relevant photographs and headlines from magazines and newspapers. Use your imagination to create the image of what you want in life. This can then be ceremonially burned or buried in the ground as an offering to the Universe, or kept in a sacred place.

Writing Rituals

As a rule of thumb, the following coloured inks should be used:

blue: Healing, mental powers, communication, messages of protection

red: Sex, courage, energy

black: Banishing rituals

green: Prosperity, abundance, fertility

The Athame And The Magical Knife

Traditionally, the athame was a ceremonial sword, around 30 in. (76 cm.) long and shaped like a sabre. Being the representation of air, it was, and still is, used to direct and control the energy of spells, in a way similar to the wand. It was used to draw a sacred circle 9 in. (23 cm.) in diameter, in which the spell is cast, and to banish any unwanted spiritual entities that might be lurking. Its symbolism derives from cabbalistic magic handed down through Jewish tradition. It was claimed in the ancient magical text (dating from around the tenth century) and known as The Sword of Moses that by using cabbalistic rituals "every wish is fulfilled and every secret revealed, and every miracle, marvel, and prodigy is performed."

Throughout the centuries the athame has been used by high priestesses to conduct a very special ceremony called "Drawing down the Moon," in which the power of the moon enters the priestess, who then becomes the vessel of the moon goddess, Isis, and able to embody her energy.

Magical knives are much easier and safer, and are traditionally used to cut herbs and plants for making incenses and herbal remedies. They should be wrapped in a white cloth and kept in a safe place until needed. The knife should either be made of silver, representing the moon, or have a black wooden handle (signifying darkness) and a sharp steel blade (illumination).

Clothing

Some witches, especially high priestesses, like to don special ceremonial robes in order to conduct their rituals, because they add authority and intensity to the ceremony. Others believe that "sky-clad" (naked) is the only way to appear because clothing dissipates energy. Being naked also represents a return to innocence and purity. If you are clothed, it is best to wear natural fibers when conducting magic ceremonies because they represent the earth elements. Witches also usually go barefoot or wear sandals made of leather, which is another representation of the natural elements.

It is interesting to trace the origins of ceremonial dress back to ancient times, particularly in areas of Central America. It is recorded that women and birds were regarded there as the interconnection with the God-force, and some priests even promoted the idea of skinning a woman in one piece, and then wearing her skin under a crown of bird feathers to celebrate the mother symbol of God – some symbol!

In Jewish traditions, the vestments of the rabbi are particularly fascinating, because they symbolize the four levels of man: the rabbi's body represents the physical shell; the undergarment, the soul; the overgarment, the spiritual aspects of man; and the golden-threaded ephod or surplice, the divine aspects of man.

To most people, the witch's apparel is as black as her soul. This image is another legacy of the puritanical times of the

Dark Ages. Black is the colour of secrets, and it is interesting to look at the psychology of wearing black garb. Those who wear black often subconsciously find it hard to identify who they are, and this is why it is so popular with teenagers. Some wear it to mirror the threatening and menacing darkness of their soul; some because black is associated with authority and tradition. To others it represents the baser sexual desires.

But witches generally love nature and the great outdoors and therefore favour colour. In fact, you are highly unlikely to meet a white witch bedecked in somber colours unless, of course, she wishes to deflect negativity or invoke invisibility.

The Pointed Hat
Did you know that the pointed hat was an invention of the Christian Church? In medieval days it was called a steeple-crowned hat, derived from the "steeple house," the Puritans'

word for a church. These hats were placed on the heads of heretics and witches by the Inquisition before they were burned, in the hope that the symbol of the church would draw salvation into their souls.

The Grimoire, or Book of Shadows

One of the most important attributes of any witch is her grimoire – the witch's personal book for recording spells, rituals, incantations and brews, herbal and incense recipes.

Grimoires date back to ancient Jewish mystical practices, the most famous of which is described in the Key of Solomon, said to have been written by King Solomon, himself a legendary magical master. It is said that God bestowed upon Solomon a magical ring so that he alone could control man, spirit, and nature, and then showered him with wisdom, riches, and honors to surpass all other men. Two other famous grimoires are the *Necronomicon*, written by an Arab named El Hazzared, and the *Sacred Book of Magic of Abra-Melin the Mage*, whose teachings are said to have been given to Moses by God.

Always handwrite your recipes and information in blue ink (signifying communication) and keep your grimoire safe. Traditionally, witches would copy bits from other witches' grimoires, adding their own pieces on the way, so that no grimoire was exactly the same. It was also a rule that the book would be burned on the death of the witch to protect her relatives from persecution. The name Book of Shadows reflects that other world beyond the veil of life, which abounds with spirits, divas, angels, and magical creation. To any witch, this physical life can be only a shadow of those wonders.

The Familiar

The puritanical Christian of medieval times was convinced that witches could not possibly work alone, that any animal that lived with a suspected witch – especially cats, toads, rats, and dogs – was nothing short of a demon-helper in disguise. It was said that these "familiars" were fed by the blood of the witch, so if any blemish or wart was found on the skin of the accused, it was immediately taken for a secret teat, and she was instantly doomed. Cats were often burned with the witch, because it was said that these animals could change shape at will in order to wreak the havoc invoked by the witch.

Hares were often tarred with the same brush, principally because they could run so fast, and seldom in a straight line. They were witches in disguise – and should be shot with a silver bullet.

Witches do, in fact, work with the diva energies of earth, air, fire, and water, purely because they respect and revere the wonders of nature. They know that trees and plants contain a vital life force, which is guarded by invisible beings such as sprites, gnomes, and fairies. Stones too vibrate with their own form of life and are likewise guarded by diva entities, who help to create the magic in our Universe.

The Besom

The broomstick, or besom as it should correctly be named, goes together with a witch like the proverbial horse and carriage. The staff, traditionally made out of ash for protection, is the representation of the male principle, and the brush, made from birch twigs for protection, exorcism, and purification, is the female principle. It is bound with a branch from the willow for protection, healing, and love. Due to its sexual symbolism, the word "besom" was adopted as slang to describe a girl with loose morals.

Originally however, the besom was made from the broom plant (hence the name broomstick) and sold by street vendors as a lucky charm to ward off evil. It was commonly used during pagan wedding ceremonies. The couple "jumped the besom" to symbolize their common-law union, while gypsy couples would jump backward and forward over it to draw in fertility blessings on their marriage.

The besom's foremost use, of course, is to enable the witch to get from A to B. Most illustrations show the

> The broomstick, or besom, goes together with a witch like the proverbial horse and carriage

witch sitting on her stick with the brush behind her. This is quite wrong. Because of its sexual significance, the brush should be ahead and, since she flies at night, her cat needs a place up front in order to give directions. Another equally important use is to ward off evil by sweeping out negativity from a room, or by clearing the magic circle of uninvited entities before you commence ritual work. Should you wish to call up a storm, place the besom in a cauldron of water and stir deasil (clockwise), or widdershins (anticlockwise) to stop it.

The Cauldron

In days of yore everyone cooked over open fires, so the cauldron was really the forerunner of the saucepan. However, its magical significance goes way back into legend. Its shape represents mother nature, in which all things are contained, and its three legs the triple face of the moon goddess. Its practical use incorporates the four natural elements – water to fill it, the earth elements of herbs, roots, and plants to cook in it, scented vapor (air element) to rise from it, and fire to boil it. Potions and brews were produced from the cauldron as if by magic to heal all ails, which is why it became synonymous with the image of the witch. It is also suggested that the cauldron, the symbol of transformation and container of the great mystery of woman and nature, was actually the original Holy Grail that King Arthur and his knights so desperately sought.

The cauldron's shape represents mother nature, in which all things are contained, and its three legs the triple face of the moon goddess

The word "cauldron" is derived from the latin *caldus* meaning hot, and the Sanskrit *cra*, to boil. The word *caudle* also comes from the same

Sanskrit root and is a sort of spiced healing gruel – nowadays fed mainly to the ill, but in earlier times made for those in childbirth and for those who came to admire the baby.

The Wand

Every witch, and fairy for that matter, is joined at the hip to her wand. It

The wand represents the element of air and evokes the energy of the spell, sending it in whichever direction the wand is pointed

represents the element of air and evokes the energy of the spell, sending it in whichever direction the wand is pointed. The wand's action relates to the arrow or lance of the ancient warrior – as it flies through the air, it carries your intent. The word "wand" derives from the Gothic word *windan*, meaning "wind" or "bind" – in magic-making, wands are used to bind the energy of the spell together.

Wands are normally made from the wood of living trees: the hazel or the elder being the best for all-purpose magic-making; willow for enhancing your wish and for working with the energies of the moon; rowan for healing and protection; ash for prosperity; oak for strength and endurance; apple for binding love. If you wish, you can tie a crystal to the top of the wand, and decorate it with runic symbols.

Some Native American tribes ask the permission of the tree before removing twigs, leaves, or branches as a mark of respect to the spirit of the tree, and they always make an offering of thanks at its base in the form of sacred herbs or tobacco. They believe that just as you take something, you should give something back. This custom is also practiced in witchcraft, for the very same reasons.

Part 3:

Practicing Witchcraft

Magical Charms and Symbols

Signs and Symbols

It is difficult to draw a clear distinction between a sign and a symbol, because over time the two words have become synonymous. However, on tracing them back to their roots, "sign" comes from the Latin *signum* meaning to mark (as in sign-ature), while "symbol" is derived from the Greek *mallein*, meaning to throw together or to compare. Both words, however, represent a non-verbal shorthand or coded language for those who recognize them.

Before man could write, he could draw – so signs and symbols have been used as a form of communication since the earliest times. Cave drawings and other objects such as pottery and jewellery bearing symbolic markings, have allowed us to discover much about the origins of mankind. And from these hieroglyphics our own alphabets and languages began to evolve. The Chinese script is a direct descendant of such symbols. Each one of the thousands of Chinese characters, is a pictograph – a picture used as a symbol in picture-writing.

Signs and symbols enable us to communicate with each other when words cannot suffice. Think of the times when you've been abroad in a country whose language is unknown

> **Music is the most powerful language on Earth because it speaks to us on a higher plane than the spoken language**

to you. More often than not, you can make your point by using signs and symbols. The hand-sign language of the deaf provides the same depth of communication as using spoken words, and the Braille alphabet allows the blind person to read as fluently as a sighted person.

Music is the most powerful language on Earth because it speaks to us on a higher plane than the spoken language. It incites emotional responses within our bodies that few spoken words can do, and people without a single word in common can together produce the most wonderful sounds by interpreting the symbolic notes from a musical score that is universally understood. In short, signs and symbols talk to us in codes, some of which are immediately decipherable, and others not. It depends whether you hold the key to the code. This is why many of the ancient sacred religious orders, like the Knights Templar and the Rosicrucians, created their own signs and symbols, which could not be interpreted by others who were wishing to infiltrate their ranks.

Aside from secret languages, signs and symbols are also used to represent a collective identity. There are few businesses without a symbolic logo that reflects its services or products. Likewise, flags immediately enable us to identify different countries or states. Road signs let us know what maneuver to make. And all of us recognize the symbolism of the Christian Cross, irrespective of our religious beliefs.

In ritual magic dating back to pre-Christian times, extremely potent symbols, numerological combinations and magical scripts were designed to resonate with the cosmic forces to draw in their energy and enhance the power of the invocation. These are still used in many forms of witchcraft, although the most popular are runes, the tarot, and astrological symbolism, which are used as a form of divination.

The Runes

I know of no other advice than this:
Go within and scale the depths of your being
from which your very life springs forth.

Rainer Maria Rilke, 1875–1926

It is said that the Scandinavian god Odin hung himself from a tree for nine days and nights to receive the wisdom of the world. Writing was known only to a few, so this knowledge appeared in symbolic characters at the base of the tree, carved on pieces of wood. Since then runic signs have been used as a form of divination similar to the tarot. The word "rumor" derives from this, because the original meaning of "rune" was "whisper" or "murmur". As such, it also stands for mystery.

Below are a few of the more popular runic symbols, but I would recommend further study, because the runic language and written script are a joy to work with. It is very easy to make your own rune set, either by painting the glyphs on a set of stones, or by carving them into pieces of wood.

↗	strength	protection	Y
✳	prosperity	abundance	☼
▽	joy	lust/sex	✕
⋈	love	healing	⟟
ß	fertility	good health	⌐

The Tarot

> The aim of life is self-development. To realize one's
> nature perfectly – that is what each of us is here for.
> People are afraid of themselves nowadays. They
> have forgotten the highest of all duties,
> the duty that one owes to one's self.

Oscar Wilde, 1854–1900

The origins of the tarot are unknown, although some people
believe that it came out of Babylonia, others out of China or
India. The earliest known record occurred around 1392 at the
court of King Charles VI of France.

In the eighteenth century the tarot found a champion in a
clergyman called Antoine Court de Gebelin, who became
convinced that it was linked to the ancient mystical

teachings of Thoth, the Egyptian god of magic and healing. Later still, the tarot became a representation of the Hebrew cabbalist teachings depicting the twenty-two pathways on the Tree of Life. The Hebrew word tora stands for the scroll on which the Pentateuch – the first five books of the Old Testament, which contain the origins of humanity and the spiritual laws by which mankind should live – were written.

It is believed that originally the twenty-two cards of the Major Acarna, which correlate directly with the twenty-two paths of the Cabbala, may have been separate from the four fourteen-card suits of the Minor Acarna, which depict the four natural elements of life and man: air/ intellect; earth/materialism; fire/ inspiration; water/emotions. When they joined forces is still a mystery. Nevertheless they are now one, making seventy-eight cards in all. The Major Arcana reflects the important events in a person's life, while the Minor Acarna adds and expands details.

Many people fear the tarot simply because, like the practice of witchcraft, it has been associated with the black arts. But used with reverence, the tarot acts as a mirror, clearly indicating the soul's progression toward enlightenment. It is a wonderful aid to self-empowerment, which leads you to discover the riches of trusting your intuition.

Astrology

A physician without a knowledge of astrology
has no right to call himself physician.

Hippocrates, ca. 460–370 b.c.

Astrology is the root of the anatomical, physiological, and metaphysical make-up of man reflected back through the individual properties of the heavenly bodies. It is the map of the soul's path during its incarnation, with all its trials and tribulations, joys and adventures, encapsulated within the wheel of life, just as the body encapsulates the soul. There are twelve astrological signs through which the soul can choose to incarnate itself, depending on the experience it needs in order to grow, with the planetary influences adding a bit of spice!

The twelve signs are divided into four elemental triangles, or Grand Trines, as they are known: earth/practical, air/cerebral, fire/enthusiasm and water/sensitive. The triangle is considered to be the oldest occult symbol in the known world because it represents:

1. The male (the sun)

2. The female (the moon)

3. The physical manifestation of that union (Jupiter)

When the zodiac is drawn out, it becomes clear that the polar-opposite sign plays an important balancing role (for example, the first sign, Aries, is balanced by the seventh sign, Libra, representing the warrior and the peace-maker respectively). The twelve signs are placed around the zodiac with the planets falling into different "houses," depending on their position in the heavens at

The Twelve Astrological Signs

1. Aries
"I am" Fire/Mars
Male principle/war
Lesson: Needs to learn
sensitivity to others and
patience.

2. Taurus
"I have" Earth/Venus
Creativity/love
Lesson: Needs to learn to go
beyond self-indulgence and
stubbornness.

3. Gemini
"I think" Air/Mercury
Communication/travel
Lesson: Needs to learn to go
beyond superficiality and
being two-faced.

4. Cancer
"I feel" Water/Moon
Emotions/home/mother
Lesson: Needs to learn to
go beyond self-pity and to
control the emotions.

5. Leo
"I will" Fire/Sun
Power/ego/father
Lesson: Needs to learn to
temper intolerance and
conceit.

6. Virgo
"I analyze" Earth/Mercury
Writing/healing
Lesson: Needs to overcome
fastidiousness and
hypercriticism.

7. Libra
"I balance" Air/Venus
Female principle
Lesson: Needs to learn to
climb off the fence and gain
confidence.

8. Scorpio
"I desire" Water/Pluto
Transformation
Lesson: Needs to overcome
jealousy, envy, secrecy, and
base sexual desire.

9. Sagittarius
"I perceive" Fire/Jupiter
Expansion/knowledge/law
Lesson: Needs to learn to
temper extravagance and
restlessness.

10. Capricorn
"I use" Earth/Saturn
Karma/discipline
Lesson: Needs to learn to
ease up and relax into life.

11. Aquarius
"I know" Air/Uranus
The unexpected
Lesson: Needs to learn to
overcome rebelliousness and
perverse behavior.

12. Pisces
"I believe" Water/Neptune
Dreams/illusions/high mind
Lesson: Needs to
learn practicality and
independence.

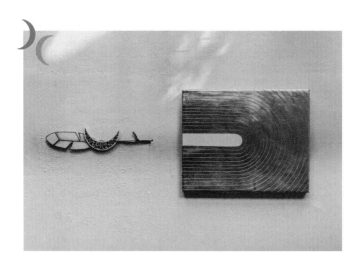

the time of the subject's birth. The sun also falls into a particular house, depending on the time of birth.

Divide a circle into four equal parts. The horizontal line becomes the ascendant, as the sun rises over the horizon around six o'clock in the morning, and its opposite becomes the descendant, where the sun sets around six in the evening. (There are summertime adjustments to be made.) The vertical line in the top half of the circle becomes noon, while the one in the lower half becomes midnight. From this, it is fairly easy to work out approximately which sign your sun falls in, even if you haven't got access to astrological data.

> Astrology is the map of the soul's path during its incarnation, encapsulated within the wheel of life, just as the body encapsulates the soul

The ten planets (including the sun and the moon) represent different facets of our human psyche. However, each glyph is also symbolic of a much higher spiritual meaning. Each one is a variation on these three basic principles: the circle (symbolizing the spirit); the half-circle (representing the moon); and the cross (the symbol of the Earth).

As life progresses year by year and the slower outer planets in the heavens transit over the natal planets of our birth charts and "fire" them into action, an internal time-clock is set off in the soul. Depending on the planets involved, it may be the right time for the soul to create a new, loving relationship. Alternatively, it may need to learn the lesson of loss, through the death of a loved one or perhaps through bankruptcy. Or it may need to experience parenthood.

When the timing is right, the Universe creates the necessary human experience. This is why life continually ducks and dives, and why it is far wiser to open your arms to change than to resist it. You cannot defy your soul's destiny to learn. That is why we are here!

Magical Numbers

Omnia innumeria sita sunt.
Everything lies veiled in numbers.

Ancient Adage

The use of numbers in magic is its cornerstone of power. But, first, a little history about the well-known father of modern-day mathematics.

Pythagoras, born around 590 b.c. and named after Pythasis, the Oracle of Delphi at the time, was to become known to his

> In the old days each measurement was aligned not only with planetary powers but also with earth energies

disciples as the "divine one." In his late teens he embarked on a spiritual quest, a journey that took thirty years of traveling all over the Middle East, Greece, parts of northern Africa and India, where he studied with important religious and esoteric teachers and healers to find the mystery of "The Hidden Light." He came to see mankind as living in three worlds: the natural, the human, and the divine, and it was he who coined the word "Philosopher," meaning lover of wisdom.

Around 530 b.c., at the age of fifty, he settled in the Greek colony of Croton in southern Italy, where he founded the first university in history, open to both men and women. Each student was dedicated to the release of his soul through purification, meditation, vegetarianism, and silence. It was here that Pythagoras taught his students the hidden wonders of the divine essence of the cosmos, the science of number vibrations, the musical harmonies of the heavenly spheres, the theory of magnitude in relation to planets and the Earth (that is astronomy), sacred geometry, and what he is remembered for today – mathematics.

Eventually Pythagoras became a liability to the authorities, who assassinated him, persecuted many of his followers, and burned down all his schools and libraries around 495 b.c. Those followers who survived kept his secrets, either passing them down through word of mouth or secretly writing them on manuscripts, which were kept hidden.

Pythagoras followed the theory that "Nothing can exist without Numbers," and the study of numbers came to be considered the origin of all things – the link to understanding the greater knowledge of God.

The Jewish cabbalastic system was based on the science of numbers, and the Old Testament is peppered with numerological references and codes, which few people can decipher. The Freemasons, it is said, founded their society on the science of numbers, as did the sacred Order of the Priory of Sion, the Knights Templar, and the Rosicrucians. Many great philosophers and scientists, including Plato and Socrates, followed the doctrines and mathematical methods of Pythagoras.

So when you were monosyllabically recounting, "The square on the hypotenuse of a right-angled triangle is equal to the sum on the squares of the other two sides," you were in fact an unwitting student of the greatest scientist, mathematician, psychic, philosopher, and magician the world has ever known.

Numbers were regarded as the divine mystery and the core to every branch of symbolism known to man. In fact not a single man-made structure could be created without them, for numbers also give us measurements. In the old days each measurement was aligned not only with planetary powers but also with earth energies, hence the awesome and exacting science of sacred geometry.

Magic-making normally uses a combination of odd numbers – 1 (the masculine), 3 (expansion), 5 (communication), 7 (spiritual love), 9 (sexual energy) – because they stand for creativity, inspiration, and adventure. They expand things, and push things forward, literally altering the course of nature.

Your Personal Magical Number

Everyone is born with their own personal magical number, which is the key to their creative expression on Earth. It is through this vibration that you learn and work until your death. Because of this, it is either your greatest strength or your greatest struggle, depending on how much you grow in self-awareness.

Numbers were regarded as the divine mystery and the core to every branch of symbolism known to man

Finding your personal number is simple. All you have to do is add your birth dates together (this is a system that dates back to Pythagoras). See opposite for an example of how to calculate this.

Finding Your Personal Number

Birth date: November 18, 1990

11th month: $(1 + 1) = 2$
18th day: $(1 + 8) = 9$
Year 1990: $1 + 9 + 9 + 0 = 19 (1 + 9) = 10 = (1 + 0) = 1$

Total: $2 + 9 + 1 = 12 (1 + 2) = 3$

The personal number is 3

Here is a guideline to the qualities of each
personal number. For further information
on how these numbers express themselves,
see the section on Creating Abundance.

number	qualities	ruled by
1	Ambition/courage	Sun
2	Emotion/harmony/cooperation	Moon
3	Creativity/joy	Jupiter
4	Will/discipline/construction	Uranus
5	The group/freedom/expansion/ communication	Mercury
6	Love/wisdom/the voice/responsibility	Venus
7	Higher learning/spirituality/ quietness	Neptune
8	Divine law/authority/materialism	Saturn
9	Unconditional service/philanthropy	Mars

Amulets

Amulets are personal charms, worn generally around the neck for healing and protection, and they work by absorbing negative energies. They can also be trees or plants that possess magical protection qualities, which are planted near a house to avert danger and evil influences.

It is said that the literal translation of the word "amulet" is "a carrying thing," originating from an old Arabic word describing a sword belt carried over the shoulder, and also a small Koran worn as a charm around the neck to ward off evil. However, the word is most likely to have derived from the Latin *amolior*, meaning to repel or drive away.

From what has been discovered from artefacts, it is obvious that most of the ancient cultures of the world created their own versions of amulets as a protection against evil forces. Egyptian warriors wore a scarab signet ring as an emblem of resurrection and immortality, and it seems everyone revered the famous all-seeing Eye, symbol of the god of the pole star, around which the heavens revolved. Early Christians wore fish amulets called Ichthus, being the first letters of the Greek words Iesous, Christos, Theou, Uious, Soter – meaning Jesus Christ, Son of God, Savior.

Most ancient cultures of the world created their own versions of amulets as a protection against evil forces

The healing and protection properties of crystals, which include precious and semi-precious stones, have been used as powerful amulets since man first discovered them glittering on the surface of the Earth. Crystals radiate different types of

energy and information, according to their characteristics of colour, shape, and density; each one is also aligned with a planetary energy.

The elements of gold and silver are the masculine and feminine conductors that reflect the male and female principles throughout our world, and out into the Universe. They are our sun and moon on Earth.

Gold represents the masculinity of the sun god Ra, and therefore the virtues of nobility, purification, wealth, strength, positivity, courage, luck, and opportunity. It stimulates actions and is used as a powerful healing aid, especially in the treatment of arthritis. Gold rings or bracelets should be worn on the right hand.

Silver, on the other hand, represents the femininity of Isis, the moon goddess. As such it emanates mothering, nurturing, wisdom, mystical dreams and visions, spiritual understanding, and romantic love. Its properties induce peacefulness and meditative states. Silver rings or bracelets should be worn on the left hand.

Amulets or charms as they are more commonly known, are more potent when they are given to you by a friend. It is the gesture of loving goodwill that empowers the charm.

Talismans

For as long as man has lived on the planet, talismans have been used as magical charms to attract wealth, harmony, and happiness, as opposed to amulets, which repel or protect. In fact, during Roman times, such was the demand for talismans that special factories were set up throughout the Empire to produce vast numbers of them.

Some people say that the word "talisman" can be traced back to the Sanskrit root *tri* meaning to pass over or fulfill. Others believe, however, that it comes from the Greek word *telesma* meaning mystery or initiation, from which in turn comes the Arabic word *tilsam*, signifying a magical image.

Talismans generate a positive force for a specific reason, desire, or goal – such as healing, prosperity, or to attract a love affair – and therefore usually last for only a limited period of time. The old lores say this is 101 days, a year and a day, or three, five, seven, or nine years. Once the goal or wish has been achieved, the energy of the talisman is finished and it should be thrown into the sea or buried in the ground.

> Talismans generate a positive force for a specific reason, desire, or goal and therefore usually last for only a limited period of time

Talisman Associations

Sun
Sunday, gold
Good fortune, hope, money

Moon
Monday, silver
Home, fertility, childbirth,
women

Mars
Tuesday, iron
Courage, sexual energy,
men, matrimony

Mercury
Wednesday, mercury
Communication, travel,
writing, the arts

Jupiter
Thursday, tin
Wealth, business, legal
matters, desires

Venus
Friday, copper
Love, romance, music, the
environment

Saturn
Saturday, lead
Property, protection, life's
pathway

Talismans usually work best when they are handmade from natural materials such as rocks, crystals, wood, and, in particular, metals that correspond to particular days of the week and their planetary energies.

For example, if you want a talisman for a business deal, you could make it from tin on a Thursday night during the waxing moon; alternatively, you could draw the glyph of Jupiter on a piece of paper or carve it on a piece of wood. Use your imagination and have some fun with this. It is advisable always to substitute the glyph of mercury for the actual metal, because mercury itself is extremely toxic!

Although talismans and amulets come in all shapes and sizes, witches are particularly partial to the pentagram and the Egyptian ankh, the origins of which I will now endeavor to explain. I have also tried to dispel the negative connotations of the serpent and the number 666.

The pentagram: This five-pointed star was considered one of the most sacred symbols of ancient times. In fact, it was the secret sign of those initiated into the Pythagorean teachings, which were aligned with those of Thoth, champion of Nut and Isis.

Apart from other, deeper occult meanings, the pentagram represents Man as the five points of the star that unite the five senses. In Christian symbolism, it defines the five points where Christ was wounded on the Cross. And to the Muslims, the pentagram is the symbol that represents marriage.

Pointed downward, it joins the infernal forces. Pointed upward, it unites with the heavens. When worn as an amulet, placed on an altar, or drawn in the air with a wand or athame, it evokes powerful protection forces. Drawn in different combinations, it is also used to invoke the power of the archangels.

The ankh: The Egyptians regarded the ankh – a cross with a loop for its upper arm – as their most sacred symbol, representing perpetual life. The loop placed on top of the cross of matter signifies the gateway through which creative power can manifest in the physical plane. The symbol of Venus is derived from the ankh – the triumph of spiritual love over base matter. So the ankh also represents the connection between humanity and the divine spirit.

The serpent:

> And the Lord said unto Moses: Take thee
> a fiery serpent and set it upon a pole and it
> shall come to pass that everyone that is
> bitten when he looketh upon it shall live.

Numbers 21:8

Before the rise to power of the Christian Church, the snake was considered to be the symbol of power, wisdom, and healing, because, apart from other mystical feats, it could disappear into the Underworld to receive messages from the dead. The serpent's head represents the Omega and its tail the Alpha (the beginning and the end), and its energy, the vital life force or Kundalini energy. As such, the snake is also a representation of sexuality.

The caduceus, emblem of the medical profession, consists of two snakes entwined on a vertical staff, representing the alchemical energies of Yin and Yang. Someone who transmutes their negative programmeing into positive self-healing is able to balance their inner male and female energy, awaken the Kundalini energy, stored at the base of the spine, and thus be led to spiritual enlightenment.

The metaphysical message of a snake being able to transmute its own poison carries the deeper meaning of "Physician, heal Thyself." To overcome the fear of snakes is to enter into a profound healing experience. It's time to reinstate the snake!

666 – The mark of the beast:

Let him that hath understanding count the number of the beast: For it is the number of man and his number is six hundred and three score and six.

Revelations 13:8

Most people have been taught to shudder with fear at the sight of the so-called devil's mark of 666. However, there really is nothing to fear. Let me explain: 6 is ruled by Venus, the planet of love and femininity. When multiplied by 3 (6+6+6) it comes to 18; 1+8 = 9, and 9 is ruled by Mars, the male energy; 9 is of course also the reverse number of 6. The masculine 9 and the feminine 6 symbolize Adam and Eve. By adding the female number of 6 to the male number of 9 we arrive at the number 15. The 15th tarot card depicts the devil or beast. The test that every man and woman has to face in a physical body is animal passion. Transform this energy into a higher creative force and we can overcome the devil within, and so move on to a higher level of spiritual understanding and sexual expression.

> Most people have been taught to shudder with fear at the sight of the so-called devil's mark of 666. However, there really is nothing to fear

Sachets or Charm Bags

Witches also make and use sachets to empower their charms. These offer especially good protection for the home or vehicle. To make a sachet to protect you or a friend while driving, place a mixture of protection herbs (see p.35) on a piece of cloth on a Wednesday (the day that corresponds to travel, see p.87). Draw the runic sign for protection and place it among the herbs, together with a quartz crystal or any other coloured crystal used for protection. Gather up the four corners of the cloth, and tie them firmly together with a piece of blue thread, cord, or string. Blue is the colour of healing and protection. Knot it five times, which signifies the number of Mercury, the guardian of travellers.

If you wish to make a protection sachet for your home, do so on a Monday (the day that corresponds to the home) and place it on your altar for two days and two nights (the number of the moon that rules the home) before hanging it over your doorway.

A fertility sachet should also be made on a Monday, using green cord, and tying the knot twice; a love sachet on a Friday, using pink or red cord, and tying the knot six times; healing sachets on a Sunday, using blue cord, and tying the knot seven times; abundance sachets on a Thursday, using green cord, and tying the knot eight times; and so on.

Plackets

Plackets (or pockets) are created specifically for placing on your altar. They are made out of two squares of material sewn together along the sides and bottom edge, leaving the top open. The dimensions of the square need to be large enough to hold a couple of photographs. Felt is ideal, because it is

available in primary colours and is very easy to work with, although you may want to use other types of material as well.

Of course you can also use a combination of two colours – one on each side of the placket – depending on what you want to effect. Here are some examples:

To make a healing placket: Make an envelope out of blue material and place a photograph of the sick person, a lock of their hair, or some other object, such as a specimen of writing, inside the placket. Empower the placket with healing thoughts and then place it on your altar. Light a blue candle and allow it to burn down completely. Keep the placket on the altar until the person is fully recovered.

To help make up a quarrel: Make a placket of pink and/or blue (for healing) and place the photographs of the quarrelsome pair face-to-face inside the envelope. In your mind's eye see them in complete harmony. Place the placket on your altar for five days and nights (the number of communication and healing) and hope they make up quickly.

To draw sexual love to you: Make a placket out of a vibrant red material, and place inside it a glyph of Mars or Venus – depending on your own preference. Light a red candle, put the placket on your altar for twenty-one days and stand back! Remember: never manipulate another person against their will. It will rebound on you with ten times as much force.

To encourage world peace: Make a placket out of blue and white material, placing inside it a picture of the world, together with other relevant photographs – perhaps of trees, dolphins, whales, or war-ravaged areas. Light a white candle to peace every evening for as long as you wish, and spend a few moments radiating healing thoughts out to the world.

There are endless uses for plackets and you can make up one according to your own desires. Each day you should enhance your placket with positive thoughts, taking time to concentrate for a few moments on what you are drawing to you, or wishing for someone else. Thought is a very powerful energy, so be prepared for some remarkable experiences to occur.

The Witch's Calendar

The Moon

> The moon is nothing but a circumambulating
> aphrodisiac, divinely subsidized to provoke
> the world into a rising birth-rate.
>
> *Christopher Fry, The Lady's Not for Burning*

Such is the moon's magnificence that she deserves special acknowledgment.

A witch's calendar is based around the phases of the moon, for it is the moon that lies at the centre of all witchcraft. The moon has been worshipped since time immemorial, and most witches pay homage to her through the personification of the goddess Isis. Hecate, the Greek moon goddess, is the patroness of witchcraft. Queen of the night, she rules the spirits, ghoulies, and ghosties, and haunts tombs and crossroads, accompanied by her howling dogs.

The word "moon" is connected to the Sanskrit root *me*, meaning to measure. This is because since ancient times, calendars, time, and the seasons of the year have always been set by her phases. The moon's orbit is elliptical, sometimes taking it farther away from the Earth than at other times and, because it rotates on its own axis within the same period of time as it revolves around the earth, it always presents the same face to us.

Since ancient times, calendars, time, and the seasons of the year have always been set by the moon's phases

It represents the feminine principle, the soul, the inner life of man, fertility, adaptation, the family, the wife, the nation, children, and hereditary qualities. It also symbolizes dance, music, story-telling, myth, ritual, pregnancy, sex, childbirth and growth, magic and the occult (that which is "hidden"), illusion, and reflection. It controls the ebb and flow of our ocean tides, just as it affects the ebb and flow of our emotions.

The moon completes its orbit of the earth in 27.3 days, which is why pagans have always considered there to be thirteen full moons during the year's cycle. The Druid calendar consisted of thirteen months, each with 28 days. Later an extra day was added to make up the 12-month solar calendar of 365 days. Some believed that the thirteenth sign belonged to the constellation of Arachne, the spider who spins the web of life. Far from being unlucky, the number 13 was

The moon orbits the earth in 27.3 days, which is why pagans have always considered there to be thirteen full moons during the year's cycle regarded with great reverence by the old world, because it represents the 1 of self, combined with the 3 of creativity, to manifest the 4 of material and physical form. It also correlates to the letter M – the centre of our alphabet, which has two feet firmly planted on the earth, joining the male and female principles together at its core. The thirteenth tarot card is Death, literally meaning the transformation of the old ways into the new. And bewitching hour is traditionally the hour between midnight and one o'clock (12+1=13), when the veil between the two worlds is said to be at its thinnest. No wonder the Church turned thirteen into a negative number! Yet it also explains why a coven consists of thirteen members – one representing each full moon.

The moon passes through five quite distinct phases:

1. Dark moon (not visible)

2. New moon (cresent moon)

3. Waxing moon (growing moon)

4. Full moon (fertile moon)

5. Waning moon (shrinking moon)

The dark moon is the most secretive and powerful time to consider spell-casting, although you should wait until the crescent moon is visible before conducting your ceremony. It has the power to pour light on your desire.

The waxing moon building up to the full moon is the time for calling in your desires and making them grow into manifestation. The full moon is the time for making powerful statements about how you wish your life to be. The thirteen full-moon rituals are called esbats, and during these major acts of magic and the ceremony of "Drawing down the moon" are performed. The waning moon is the time for making reducing spells (excellent for losing weight, moving from an old home, etc.) and releasing all those thoughts and situations that no longer serve you.

The Thirteen Pagan Moons

January Snow moon

February Death moon

March Awakening moon

April Grass moon

May Planting moon

June Rose moon

July Lightning moon

July/August First fruits moon

August/September Harvest moon

September/October Hunter or blood moon

October/November Tree moon

November/December Long night moon

December/January Ice moon

Elemental Symbolism

North

Element: *Earth*

*Material abundance,
fertility, work, money*

Season: *Winter*

Tarot suit: *Pentacles*

Astrological signs:
Taurus / Virgo / Capricorn

Altar Symbols:
*Flowers, herbs, earth,
crystals, stones, money*

Colour: *Green or black*

South

Element: *Fire*

*Inspiration, intuition,
creativity, change,
sexual energy*

Season: *Summer*

Tarot suit: *Wands*

Astrological signs:
Leo / Sagittarius / Aries

Altar Symbols:
*Burning candles,
incense, fire*

Colour: *Red*

East

Element: *Air*

*Intellect, clarity of
thought, messages*

Season: *Spring*

Tarot suit: *Swords*

Astrological signs:
Aquarius / Libra / Gemini

Altar symbols:
*Feather, empty bowl,
smoke of incense*

Colour: *Yellow*

West

Element: *Water*

Emotions, love

Season: *Fall*

Tarot suit: *Cups*

Astrological signs:
Scorpio / Pisces / Cancer

Altar symbols:
*Bowl or chalice of water,
sea shells*

Colour: *Blue*

The Four Elements

The witch also works closely with the four elements – air, fire, earth, and water – and the four cardinal directions – north, south, east, and west. These relate to the four holy living symbols of Ezekiel, the Old Testament visionary who prophesied to the Jews in exile in Babylonia. The four symbols are found on many great religious buildings above the main entrance, and have been incorporated into tarot symbolism by decorating "The world" – the twenty-first card of the Major Arcana. These symbols represent the fixed signs of the zodiac: air/Aquarius/man and intellect; fire/Leo/lion and inspiration; earth/Taurus/bull and materialism; water/Scorpio/eagle transcending the watery darkness of the scorpion. Christianity also equates these elements with the four evangelists: Matthew, Mark, Luke, and John.

Festival Days and Dates

The meeting of witches is known as a sabbat, and there are four major and four minor sabbats during the year cycle.

It has been suggested that the word "sabbat" comes from the Hebrew *Shabbath*, meaning sacred, or a holy time. Such was the paranoia and intolerance of Christian fanatics during the Middle Ages that, apart from burning women as witches, they also accused the Jews of unholy practices. The words "synagogue" and "sabbath" were taken from the Jewish language and applied to these so-called witches' meetings. Another school of thought suggests that "sabbat" is taken from the Greek god Dionysus's title of Sabadius. He was the god of wine, women, song, and revelry.

The meeting of witches is known as a sabbat, and there are four major and four minor sabbats during the year cycle

Days to Cast Spells

The planets govern specific days on which to perform certain magical rituals:

Sunday: sun (Leo), the sun's day
Rules success, ambition, career, sport, healing

Monday: moon (Cancer), the moon's day
Rules psychic powers, clairvoyance, home, childbirth, feminine qualities

Tuesday: mars (Aries and Scorpio), Tiw's day
Rules courage, men, sexual energy, war

Wednesday: mercury (Gemini and Virgo), Woden's day
Rules communication, education, travel, mental agility, writing, acting

Thursday: jupiter (Sagittarius), Thor's day
Rules expansion, wealth, political power, law, business, insurance matters

Friday: venus (Libra and Taurus), Freya's day
Rules love, beauty, music, the arts, the environment

Saturday: saturn (Capricorn), Saturn's day
Rules karma, property, inheritance, agriculture

The four main sabbats were a time for local villages to gather together to celebrate the four most important seasonal changes in the year. This was also a time for cleansing the old, and for welcoming in the new, by lighting great "bane" or "bone" fires, which were made from accumulated refuse and bones.

The Four Main Sabbats

Samhaine

31 October (also known as Allhallows Eve)

Samhaine marks the end of one witches' year and the beginning of the next. With it comes the onset of winter, when the leaves begin to fall. Catching thirteen leaves, one for each full moon of the coming year, guarantees to bring you love, abundance, and joy. This was also regarded as the time when dead souls came back to life. The fire festival served to light the path of departed souls to the other side.

Imbolc

2 February (also known as Candlemas)

> If Candlemas Day be dry and fair
> The half o' winter's come and mair;
> If Candlemas Day be wet and foul
> The half o' winter was gone at Youl.

Old proverb

Imbolc signifies the halfway point between midwinter and the spring equinox, and celebrates the purity and innocence of the virgin maiden. This is symbolized by delicate white snowdrops and new shoots appearing in the ground. Traditionally, this festival was the time when all the candles for the coming year would be made, to symbolize the light coming out of the darkness. Imbolc is the time to state your objectives for the year ahead and to do fertility dances, either for yourself or for the crops!

Beltaine

30 April (also known as May Eve)

This is an old Celtic festival, when cattle were driven between bel-fires as an act of purification and protection from disease, or as a prelude to sacrifice. More importantly, spring has sprung and it is a time for frivolity. Country folk used to bedeck their homes with May blossom and wear posies in their hair. To mark the festival a maypole was erected as a symbol of virility, decorated with garlands of white and red flowers, topped with a sprig of broom to symbolize the blood and milk of the maiden goddess, and danced around by the villagers to celebrate the beginning of summer.

Lagnasad

1 August (also known as Lammas)

Lammas marks the time of harvest thanksgiving – when the first fruits were offered to the earth goddess in gratitude for a successful harvest, and farm laborers would go to "wakes" held to honour and mourn the death of the corn king. Through his selfless sacrifice, the corn could be made into new bread and milled into flour, to be stored for winter use. This is a winding-down stage toward winter and therefore a time to take stock of dreams and ambitions. New plans and changes can be formulated for the following years during the long dark days of winter.

The four main sabbats were a time for local villages to gather together to celebrate the four most important seasonal changes in the year

The Four Minor Sabbats

The Solstices

These occur when the sun reaches its most northern and southern points during its elliptical path and appears to stand still, before returning on its course. The two solstices mark the turning points of the year, and are therefore extremely important dates in the witch's calendar.

Winter Solstice

(Yule) 21 December

This marks the shortest day of the year. Daylight hours subsequently become longer.

Summer Solstice

(Midsummer) 21 June

The longest day of the year. Daylight hours subsequently become shorter.

The Equinoxes

These occur when the sun passes across the equator, making night and day equal across the globe.

Eostre or vernal equinox

(spring) 21 March

The world is quickening for the time of birth.

Michaelmas

(autumn equinox) 29 September

The last of the harvest, and the preparation for winter.

Casting a Sacred Circle

To understand the symbolism of the sacred circle, we need to retrace our steps to earlier times. And why not start at Stonehenge, which was built from around 2000 b.c. Evidence shows that it was an extraordinary timepiece – a precise astronomical clock and cosmic calculator, which followed the cyclical movement of the moon, planetary constellations and the sun. Many stone circles throughout the world were constructed for this purpose, as well as being sacred sites in which to conduct dedicatory and celebratory rituals.

In those days astronomy and astrology were one and the same thing. What we know today as the zodiac – taken from the Greek word *zoidiakos* meaning "signal" or "circle" and incorporated into the word *ziodion*, meaning "animal circle" – developed from the study and practice of those arts. It is interesting to observe that most animals curl up in a circle to

sleep, and that birds automatically construct their nest in a circular shape.

Virtually all early civilizations revered the shape of the circle for what it represented – ultimate cosmic order. It was believed that the Universe was held together by a thread, or binding force, depicted as the ouroboros, the snake swallowing its own tail. Thus the circle became the symbol of perfection, representing the unity of self; the seed of the fruit; the heart of man; the ovum; the womb. In Eastern traditions the circle became synonymous with the spiritual wheel of life. As two halves, it represents the conscious and subconscious; heaven and earth; nothing and all; the psyche and the Universe.

In ancient Egypt the cipher of 0 was regarded as the number of Nut, the mother of Osiris, Isis, Nephthys and Set. It was the holiest of places, from which all knowledge came; the ultimate symbol of femininity and fertility.

Some Native American tribes refer to the circle as a medicine wheel or sacred hoop. On it are placed the four cardinal directions, which represent various stages of growth and enlightenment through which the soul must pass to complete the "Good Red Road" of physical life.

The circle is the symbolic source of the life-death-life cycle, which we need to experience in order to evolve farther along the path toward higher consciousness, until we no longer desire or need to experience the human form.

Witches usually cast protective circles in which to perform their magic-making. The circle is generally 9 ft (2.7m.) in diameter, which represents the nine orders of the angels and evokes the power of Mars. The high priestess opens the circle by walking anticlockwise round it, following the path of the moon. This is called going widdershins. Alternatively, she draws the circle with her wand or athame. Incantations, chants, and prayers of blessing are then said to cleanse and purify the space before any magic work takes place. The circle is "unwound" by the priestess walking, or drawing the circle in the path of the sun, clockwise. This is known as going deosil. Some witches make their magic circle by opening it clockwise and closing it anticlockwise. It depends on local traditions and practices.

Before casting your own circle, make sure you will not be interrupted, for interruptions dissipate the flow of energy. This is sacred work and needs to be respected. Your room needs to be well-ventilated because the combination of burning herbs and

Virtually all early civilizations revered the shape of the circle for what it represented – ultimate cosmic order

oils, together with concentrated mind activity, tends to make you feel a bit "heady" after a while. Cast your circle either by walking round the circumference of your circle or by drawing it in the air with your wand or athame.

Always remember to respect the environment. This is part of the witch's code of practice

Should you wish to work in nature, again make sure that you are in a place well away from people who may chance upon you. And always remember to respect the environment. This is part of the witch's code of practice.

Incantations and Dance

Finally, a few words about the power of voice and movement. Most orthodox religions and secular beliefs use varying combinations of music, voice and movement – including the singing of hymns and intoning of psalms – to raise states of consciousness. This opens up the individual or group to a receptive or meditative state in which they are able to connect with the higher forces.

The famous whirling dervishes of the Sufi religion enter into a trance through the continual circular movements of their bodies, which stimulate the seven chakra centres, enabling them to attain blissful states of consciousness. Buddhists chant on a daily basis to release negative thought-patterns, and to gain spiritual strength. The chanting also sends out powerful healing thoughts on an astral level.

Witches chant incantations to clear their thoughts and focus their minds on the task in hand. New Age practitioners have

adopted incantations and renamed them affirmations, but in reality affirmations are evoking the power of witchcraft.

In the chapters that follow on creating love, abundance, and miracles, I have included many incantations that you may wish to use, or you may prefer to create your own for specific occasions. Always do what feels right for you.

The Witch's Way to Draw in Love

Love is the most precious gift we can give to ourselves and to each other. It allows us to grow toward our higher spiritual aspirations, and by opening our hearts, we can begin to break through our fears and negative thought-patterns. So creating the magic to manifest positive and supportive relationships in our lives is a serious matter.

First, you need to determine the type of experience you want. Is it love, or just plain lust? Could it be that you want to draw in new friends, or enhance your relationships with your family? Whatever it is, it is very important to take full responsibility for the experience you are wanting to create. Attempting to wrestle someone out of another's arms, or enticing a person to you against their will, is not practicing the craft of the wise.

How to Call in a Loving Relationship

The following ritual is specifically designed to call in a loving relationship, although you can adapt it to create other types of relationship. You may choose to carry out the ritual alone or with friends.

The perfect day to create a love spell is on a Friday, for this is ruled by Venus, the planet of love and wisdom. Choose a time when you will not be interrupted and can put energy into your ritual. There are three distinct phases of the ritual: the clearing-out ritual; the letting-go ritual; drawing in a loving relationship.

The ritual is designed to take a full cycle of the moon to complete. However, if you feel that the initial two phases are unnecessary, you can complete just the final phase.

The Altar

For your altar you will need:

Pink candles (one for each present)

Love incense

Charcoal in a heatproof container, set on
a heatproof base if using loose incense

Large heatproof dish

Your favourite flowers with which to decorate
your altar (flowers always raise the vibrations of love)

Any other personal items with which
you wish to decorate your altar

1. The clearing-out ritual

Light a pink candle to mark your commitment to creating
a new relationship. Spend a few moments just breathing
this wish deeply into your body and, as you exhale, notice
any emotions that surface. Acknowledge them, then
gently release them. Now repeat the following incantation
as many times as you wish:

Love come, flying free
Bring my perfect partner to me.

Notice how you feel toward yourself as you say this. Do you
feel "it is hopeless"; "no one could possibly love me"; "I'm
too thin/ugly/scraggy-haired"; "my relationships always
end in disaster"; "I don't trust anyone", etc? Honour those
feelings – take a piece of paper and write, "These are
my fears and self-doubts, which stop me creating a really
positive relationship" at the top. Then list your fears.

Next, clear out the north-east corner of every room in your home. According to the Chinese system of Feng Shui, this corner governs the area of relationships and marriage. Are your corners full of unwanted stuff, or perhaps they are bleak and empty? Put a luscious green plant in the space, or perhaps a reflecting crystal globe or mirror. Once you have completed your clear-out – and that includes all photographs of ex-lovers and old love letters – give your unwanted items away. Take some time to enjoy the space you have created. Does the furniture need shifting around or does anything else need to be dispensed with? Once you feel happy with your cleansing, say the following incantation three times:

Love, now there is room
Come with the tides of the moon.

You are now ready for the next step.

2. The letting-go ritual

You will need to set aside several hours to do this, preferably on a Friday evening, when the moon is waning. Switch off your phone and make sure you will not be disturbed. If you are with friends, sit together quietly in a circle to create a sacred space for you all to enjoy.

Light a pink candle, one for each person present, and some incense. Look at the piece of paper on which you listed all your doubts and fears. Do you need to add to it? Be really honest with yourself. As each feeling surfaces, give it a colour. If, for instance, you feel sadness, give it a brown or black colour; if you are feeling intense rage, give it a deep red slash. Then write beside the colour all the experiences and people that it represents. Share your fears out loud with those who are with you.

When you have finished, complete the evening by joining hands together. Put all your fears and doubts into the centre of the circle by saying them out loud, and then imagine them being transformed by beams of love from the Universe. Keep your paper with you for three days and three nights. Read and re-read it, adding to it whenever you feel it is necessary. On the third night, which will be Monday, the moon's day, set out your altar to create a sacred space. This is a very powerful ceremony and again you may need a couple of hours in which to perform it, especially if you are with friends.

Light the candles and incense, then sit quietly for a few moments. For the final time, read your list, and allow the colour of each negative thought to come into your mind's eye. Gently release them as you breathe each one out of your body. Then call each person who has been a negative influence on your life into your mind's eye and release them, by saying out loud an incantation along the following lines:

. . . . [name of person], I unconditionally forgive you for all the hurt you have caused me and I release you from my life. Thank you for the lesson, but it is time to move on! I choose to set my heart free into love, so that from this day on I draw only positive and supportive relationships to me.

Keep saying this until you feel you have really forgiven all those who have caused you hurt in the past. Now you are ready to burn your list. Light it carefully with the candle flame, place it in the heatproof dish, and watch it turn to ash. As you do so, say the following incantation:

Burn, burn
All those thoughts that churn
That stop my love from becoming alive.

Then take the ash outside and either scatter it into the night air or bury it in the ground, saying:

Go, dark thoughts
Scatter far and wide
Into the night
Be thou gone
So mote it be.

"So mote it be" is the witch's equivalent of saying "Amen" or "Blessed be."

Return to your altar and give yourself time to reflect on the magnitude of what you have done. It is hard for someone to have a healthy, loving relationship with you unless you love and respect yourself, so be proud of who you are and learn to recognize that every relationship in your life is a reflection of your own level of self-love. Those who open their hearts, to learn forgiveness of themselves and others, break free to draw in a higher conscious level of relationship.

Allow the candles to burn themselves out completely. The spell for letting go is complete. Now it is time to create that new relationship! Over the next three days, make a mental list of all the attributes you would admire in a prospective partner. Take your time.

3. Drawing in a loving relationship

This needs to be done preferably on a Friday night, during the new moon phase. Once again choose a time when you will not be disturbed. Lower the lights and make the room comfortable and restful.

Anoint either two or six pink candles with essential oils, such as patchouli and sandalwood, score them with your initials and then create your altar. Place representations of each of the four elements – air, earth, fire, and water, in the four corners, together with fresh flowers and any crystals or personal love tokens that you feel may enhance your ritual.

Taking paper and coloured pens, draw a picture of your heart. What does it have to offer you and your partner? How big is it? Is it afraid? Would you want it, if it was offered to you? Then take a second piece of paper and make a list of all the attributes you want in your prospective partner. Be specific. Make sure you ask for someone who is the right age, free of other emotional

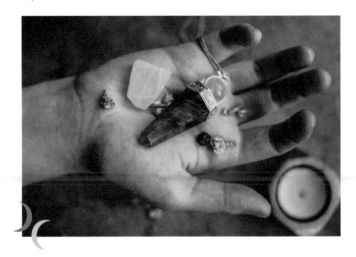

ties, and, above all, ready to enter into a committed relationship.

Place your list and drawing on your altar, then light your candles, saying the following incantation:

Draw to me my perfect mate
That I may love dear and true
Let him/her my twin soul be
And let our union bring infinite blessings
On all we do and on all we meet
So mote it be.

Repeat this three times, absorbing it into your heart, body, and soul. As you meditate on the candle flame, ask your mind's eye to give you an image of the person you are drawing to you. Then take a few moments to give thanks to your guardian angels for being with you throughout this time. You can now ceremonially burn the list and drawing, bury them, or keep them in a safe place.

Your ritual is now complete. The only thing left for you to do is to trust. Of course, it may take a little time before your perfect partner appears but if you open yourself up to signs and portents, the Universe has a funny habit of sending out little teasers just as your life is about to change.

You never can tell where, or how, you are going to meet your partner. Instead of searching blindly, my advice is to allow it to happen in its own time, to be open, acknowledge coincidences, strange feelings, and compulsions to do something different. Above all, follow your instincts, even if your friends and family tell you you're mad – because this is when the magic is calling to you.

How To Enhance Your Love Spell

You have done your spell, cleared out all your old love letters, sent your list to the Universe, and left your singleness behind at your favourite sacred sites, yet you may still feel a lingering doubt. If so, carry orris root in a green bag with you everywhere you go. Alternatively, make up a love sachet comprising a pinch of meadowsweet, ginger, dragon's blood (resin from the dragon-tree), apple blossom, jasmine, lavender, and rose. Add six drops of patchouli and sandalwood oil, together with a rose-quartz crystal. Place this sachet on your altar on a Friday night during a new moon. Leave for three days. It is then ready for you to put into a pouch, which you can either hang around your neck or carry in your handbag.

> If you open yourself up to signs and portents, the Universe has a funny habit of sending out little teasers just as your life is about to change

Another tip: always eat masses of apricots, apples, brazil nuts, capers, ginger, licorice, raspberries, strawberries, tomatoes, and peas, because these all vibrate to the energy of love.

Plant a love window box or a pot containing pansies, poppies, thyme, tulips, violets, and asters. It's a delightful experience watching your love grow and blossom. Another old wives' tale, which undoubtedly works, is to throw a shoe into a willow tree: If it stays there, start planning the wedding! However, just to make sure, you could also put couch-grass under your bed. Of course, you could just throw a tonka bean into your local river, while jumping up and down on your left leg, as you call in your wish for love. . .

How To Create Lustful Encounters
This ritual goes hand-in-hand with a warning: always practice safe sex, and be honest with your partner about your motives. Witchcraft is there to help and heal, never to hurt or harm. So, you have been warned!

Red is the colour of passion, so wear scarlet or bright-red naughty underwear; smear yourself with avocado from head

> **Always practice safe sex and be honest with your partner about your motives**

to foot, and eat it mixed with garlic and onions; drink gallons of hibiscus tea – so potent was this it thought to be that Egyptian women were forbidden to drink it.

Nettle soup is also excellent for inducing lust, as is nibbling loads of parsley, but be careful because this also promotes fertility. The Elizabethans swore by sea holly, which was boiled in sugar and eaten as sweets. Apparently mermaids used to feed on it to increase their seductive charms. The Romans used to eat lettuce after dinner to arouse their sexual ardor. And according to ancient folklore, carrying endive is also helpful, because it removes all obstacles in your path! You could also regard the good old tomato as a friend, when in need. The Spaniards who brought it back from South America and introduced it to Europe, prized its aphrodisiac properties so highly that they called it the love apple.

Finally, go hunting on a Tuesday night, because it is ruled by Mars, the god of lust. Good luck!

How To Solve Sexual Problems

Where there is sex, there can also be problems, and strange though it may seem, even witches are not exempt from these.

Chronic sexual problems usually stem from a deep-rooted anxiety, often related to negative childhood experiences, so I would always recommend that anyone suffering from sexual problems should consult a therapist or counsellor who specializes in such matters.

Often it comes down to the passion-slaying rigors of life: the kids, the shopping, the cleaning, the job. . . But with any anxiety-related problem, the most vital thing is to learn to relax. I always advocate a bath by candlelight, into which I add a drop of lavender and geranium oil. There is something wonderfully seductive about the combination of candlelight, water, and oils, especially when you're sharing your bath with your partner.

Use candlelight in the bedroom as well, and spray your sheets and pillowcases with ylang ylang oil or burn jasmine, sandalwood, patchouli, rose, or clary sage in the bedroom. All these oils have strong aphrodisiac properties. Give each other a gorgeous sensual massage and, if that doesn't work, then one partner should carry acorns in their pockets. They are said to increase sexual attractiveness and prowess, and to cure impotency. The acorn is also a powerful fertility nut, to be worn by women wishing to conceive.

Try placing some dragon's-blood under the mattress, or feed your partner beans: eating them helps to cure impotency, because they resemble testicles! Capers are also said to be excellent for lust-enactment and, as for carrots, you can't lose. Olives and avocados are two of the most potent fruits for raising the pheromones, while other lust-inducing herbs include garlic, dill, mint, rosemary, lemongrass, and parsley.

Creating Abundance

The trap that most people fall into when thinking about abundance is that they equate it with money. In reality money acts merely as a symbol, but the problem is that we have forgotten that this is all it is, and most of us have become shamefully spellbound by it.

The word "abundance" derives from the Latin *abundare*, meaning to overflow, and a heart overflowing with joy compassion, and inspiration leads to riches beyond compare. The word "money," however, dates back to Roman times, around 344 b.c. when the first Roman mint was created by an affluent man, who built a temple to the goddess Juno Moneta. The coins that came from it were thus known as moneta.

In early times, different kinds of bartering systems were used, and many cultures and religious doctrines, such as the Mosaic Laws, decreed that the first fruits of the harvest should be offered as a divine sacrifice of thanks to the deities. However, as time evolved, those who had (as opposed to those who had not) stated their claim as sovereign lords by charging for the privilege in goods and chattels. The Church also thought up ingenious ways of taxing people – and thus tithing was born. Originally, one-tenth of all that was produced on the land was given voluntarily to the Church, but by the end of the eighth century this tithe had became compulsory. These payments finally ceased around 1534, with the dissolution of the monasteries, but were simply transferred to Henry VIII, and so the endless struggle of the peasant to make enough to live on continued. Nowadays the government takes it instead, but we have become impregnated with the belief that in order to survive we have to throw ourselves onto the sacrificial treadmill. This thought-pattern has to change, if you want to overflow with abundance.

As I have already explained, your personal magical number is the guiding force concerning how your soul wishes to express itself in this life – that is, in which direction your true creative expression lies – so if you haven't already worked out your own number, do so now by turning to page 67.

Personal Magic Numbers

1s: love to champion causes and, like all great visionaries, tend to need a host of minions to clear up after them. No.1 is ruled by the sun, and therefore tends to be independent, stout of heart, courageous, and protective. But woe betide anyone who dares to threaten them. 1s are the innovators and ideas people, who love to try something new but are not very good at sharing themselves.

2s: are prone to being real softies, because they like to be surrounded by harmony and balance. They are warm-hearted, trustworthy, and diplomatic to the utmost. They are the perfect counterpart to No.1 and, because No.2 is ruled by the moon and affiliated to the sign of Libra, excellent with money. They love any form of art and craft, especially music.

3s: are creative, pure and simple and need to express themselves. They are ruled by Jupiter, the planet of expansion, and are therefore prone to do things to excess. 3s love to perform, and many become painters, actors, teachers, demonstrators, scientists, researchers, television and film writers.

4s: are the planners and constructors of life, ruled by Uranus, who love to pore over numbers and lists, columns and details. They make excellent proofreaders, accountants, draftspeople and organizers in general.

5s: are ideas people, who hate being tied down to anything remotely resembling a time schedule. Ruled by Mercury, they are the great communicators of life and love to travel far afield, making excellent explorers and adventurers. Commitment is a great problem for 5s, because there is so much out there to investigate.

6s: are born to sing! So if you are a No.6 and haven't found your voice, sign up with a singing teacher, join a choir, or learn to chant. 6s are ruled by Venus, so they are usually in love with someone, somewhere, and because they thrive on responsibility they make great doctors, nurses, ministers, healers, and homemakers.

7s: are spiritual beings, who need to take time and space to consider the effect of life, love and the Universe. Ruled over by Neptune, they like to delve into things and make good researchers, chemists, historians, astronomers, occultists, witches, wizards, and musicians. They do, however, need an enormous amount of understanding because they often find it extremely difficult to understand themselves.

8s: love being bossy and in charge of everything. They make very successful bankers and accountants, kings, business people, property tycoons, and corporate heads, and are often extremely good sportsmen, too. No.8 governs the material world and is ruled by Saturn.

9s: are life's drama-queens, ruled over by Mars. No. 9 stands for unconditional love, forgiveness, and completion, so there's rarely a dull moment around them. They adore the stage, movies, food, travel – in fact, anything that faintly resembles the broader canvas of life.

Should your personal number add up to 11, 22, 33, 44, and so on, there is no need to add the digits together, because you've hit a sort of karmic jackpot.

11s: teachers of the zodiac, visionaries, and peacemakers.

22s: architects of peace, the master-builders of the new world.

33s: vibrate to the Christ consciousness and are here to spread light and joy in dark corners.

44s: workers of Light, here to construct a more balanced world.

55s: here to break things open, to give the world a shake-up.

00s. carry responsibility for promoting health and welfare throughout the world.

77s: are the spiritual teachers, those who can raise our consciousness to greater heights.

88s: are spiritual healers and leaders, here to carry us forward into a better world.

99s: are the Liberaces of planetary reform!

Once you understand how your soul needs to express itself, you can begin to grasp the changes you need to make in order to create a more joyous life. Once you are in control of your life, the Universe will automatically throw abundance and prosperity at you.

If you're a round peg working in a square hole, get out and find a round hole. You will never find joy from making money doing something you loathe. Everyone needs to work to pay the mortgage, feed the kids, pay for a vacation, but true abundance is about quality of life. We must learn to listen to our heart when it tells us that what we are doing does not serve us. Once we hear, the door swings open and life will become abundant and fulfilling. So open that door.

How to Create Abundance

This ritual is in two parts – the clearing-out ritual and drawing in abundance – but you can skip straight to the second part if you wish. It is, however, very important to take a look at your attitude towards your own self-worth before continuing. Do you consider yourself worthy to receive the universal gifts of abundance and love, or do you subconsciously set up situations that preclude this?

1. The clearing-out ritual

As with creating a love spell, you need to clear out the old in order to let new ideas in. The perfect time for doing this ritual is on a Thursday evening, during the waning moon. Light a green candle and place with some prosperity incense on your altar.

Make a list of your fears concerning money. What does lack of it really mean to you? Then write down the worst possible thing that could happen to you if you lost the lot and were left with nothing. Let your imagination run wild. Close your eyes and let yourself feel the fear. Start to give your fear a shape and a colour, then let it out of your body. As it is released, say the following incantation:

Fly thee free
So I might see
My perfect path of creativity
Appear clearly to me
So mote it be.

Repeat this incantation until you feel the fear leaving you completely. This may take some time, and it may be appropriate to repeat the exercise over several days, or

even weeks. Then take the list of your fears and set light to it in the candle flame. Place it in a heatproof bowl on your altar and, as you watch it burn to ash, say the following incantation three times:

Burn, burn
All those thoughts that churn
To stop my creative spirit
From coming alive
So mote it be.

Sit for a while, and imagine a door opening deep within you. This is the door to your creativity, the path to your joy. Let the candle burn down completely, then scatter the ashes of your fears into the night air, or bury them in the ground, while saying:

Go fears, go
Scatter far and wide

> *Be thou gone*
> *So mote it be.*

Your clearing-out ritual is now complete. While you are waiting for the moon to reach its waxing phase, so that you can conduct part two of the ritual, clear out the north-west corner of all your rooms. These are the prosperity areas in Chinese Feng Shui. Put plants or money boxes there, a mirror or green crystals – anything that signifies abundance to you. Every time you walk into the room, be conscious that you are clearing your negative thought-patterns and are now willing to draw prosperity to you in abundance.

2. Drawing in abundance

This part of the ritual needs to be conducted on a Thursday evening, during the waxing moon. Make your altar, and decorate it with symbols of abundance, such as money, food, silver and gold jewellery, photographs of

friends, green crystals, etc. Anoint a green candle with eight drops of mint essential oil and write your name in the wax three times. Light your candle and incense.

Sit for a few moments, and open your heart to receive energy from your guides and angelic forces. When you feel ready, take a piece of paper and make a list of all the things that you wanted to do as a child, when your spontaneity was at its height. Then make a second list of all the things you would still love to do, but for which you "never have time." Make a third list of your interests and hobbies. Take your time. See what corresponds.

Then, with coloured pens, draw your perfect picture of prosperity and abundance. How do you want to create them in your life? Do you want to write a book; become an actor; run a company; become a mature student; open your own restaurant? If nothing comes immediately to mind, draw patterns with the pens and open your heart to allow a message to come to you during your dream time. All you have to do is believe in yourself. Once your picture is complete, you should say the following incantation:

Mother Earth, Father Sky
Bring me my joyous desire
Brother Sun, Sister Moon
Make it quick, make it soon
So mote it be.

Place the picture on your altar for three days and three nights, lighting an anointed green candle and incense every day. Afterwards you can keep the picture on your altar or place it in one of your prosperity corners; alternatively, you can bury it.

Before you fall asleep, ask the moon goddess – or your favourite deity – to bring you a sign to show you your way forward. Be prepared for this message to come in unexpected ways. The Universe will find a means – all you have to do is trust.

Performing these ritual spells is an extremely powerful act and may mean that you need to make a number of changes in your life in order to step onto your new path. It is difficult to break away from other people's expectations and might well upset those around you. That, however is the test. Remember that no matter how negative people are toward you, you are only a victim of your own fear of letting go.

How to Follow the Magical Laws of Tithing

This follows the same principle as offering up the "first fruits" of the harvest. You need to open two extra bank or mutual society accounts, or set aside a couple of special money pots at home. Label one "me" and the other "first fruits." Into each pot or account put 10 percent of everything that you earn, even if it's only a small amount, because those trifles do add up.

The first fruit pot: This is your unconditional give-away pot. There may be a friend who needs help in paying a bill, or perhaps you would like to give the money to charity. It doesn't matter how much you give, as long as you give unconditionally.

First fruiting teaches you to let go and trust that the Universe will provide abundantly for you. Tithing allows the natural

flow of things to happen. The more you let go of your fear of "lack," the more you will be supported.

The "me" pot: This pot is for creating your future abundance, and you can use this money only when you need something that will increase it. For example, you may want to become an artist, so you could buy your materials with it; or perhaps you need a suit for a job interview that really interests you. It is not to be dipped into to buy the latest gadget, pay the electricity bill, or to go on vacation. It is your sacred abundance pot. Treat it with reverence and it will increase and increase.

How you spend the rest of what you earn, or own is up to you. It is, however, important to constantly ask yourself how much you actually need. The Universe always provides enough; it is simply your fear that prevents it from coming to you. Just remember that a greedy soul never sleeps in peace.

How to Enhance your Abundance Spell

Wear orange and/or green underwear! These colours are bound to bring prosperity. If that's a little over the top, make a circle of eight green candles, placing them on eight silver coins face-up, then light them on a Thursday evening, during the waxing moon. You will also need to carry some almonds; and shinning up an almond tree will

make absolutely sure that you can create a multimillion take-over of whatever you want. Alternatively, you could bury a chestnut.

If you have a garden, don't kill the bindweed – its prosperity consciousness is as rampaging as its desire to throttle your flowers. Mint also attracts prosperity, and so do honesty and honeysuckle. On the other hand, you could become a culinary prosperity genius: take a handful of blackberries and a chunk of pineapple, and throw them into a bowl. Chuck in a few cashew nuts, a sprig of basil and a pinch of nutmeg. Mix together with cooked buckwheat and serve immediately. To follow, eat grapes, grapes, and more grapes. If all else has failed, don't despair.

How to Ask for a Particular Thing

So generally you're happy with your lot, but you'd still love to have just that little extra to buy a new car, or to splash out on that longed-for vacation. Magic can help with this too. It's simply a matter of logging in your particular need with the Universe. If you don't ask, how can the Universe provide?

On a Thursday night during the waxing moon, create a circle on your altar out of stones or crystals. Anoint an orange candle with three drops of almond oil and score your name in the wax three times. Then light some incense. Draw a picture of whatever it is you wish to come into your life. Empower it with prosperity symbols, photographs, headlines from newspapers, etc. Then say the following incantation:

Mother Earth, Father Fire
Bring me what I now desire.

> *Brother Sun, Sister Moon*
> *Make it quick and make it soon.*
> *So mote it be.*

Place your picture in the centre of your stone circle and leave it undisturbed for eight days and nights. On the last night, anoint a green candle with mint oil, light prosperity incense, and take a few moments to meditate on your picture. Empower it with thought and action. Then offer the picture to the candle and let it burn to ash. Bury the ash outside or in a plant pot, saying:

> *Mother Earth, take this wish*
> *Make it grow quick as quick*
> *Sister Moon, shine down on me*
> *Let this become my prosperity*
> *So mote it be.*

Now forget about it. The Universe has heard and will join forces with your spiritual helpers to manifest your desire. May I remind you, though, that your wish may not be granted in quite the way you had in mind. Rest assured that the higher forces know better than you.

How to Empower Yourself During Interviews

The pressure of performing well in an interview often creates anxiety and stress. Magic is a delightful way of calling in support from the unseen worlds to help you relax and enjoy it, rather than biting your fingernails to the bone. If possible try to arrange your interview for a Wednesday during the waxing cycle of the moon, especially when Mercury is going direct (forward) in motion rather than retrograde (backward). You can find out its movements through the astrological

columns in newspapers. Being the planet of communication, a retrograde Mercury tends to bring frustrations, hitches, and misunderstandings.

On the eve on your interview, affirm your confidence by lighting a blue candle (for communication) and anointing it with rosemary oil. Score your initials in its wax five times. Place it inside your circle of stones and leave it to burn out completely. Place a piece of green tourmaline or clear quartz in your pocket, so that you can call on its help if things become a bit tense, by holding it in your hand. Or eat some pecan nuts just before you go in, as they are sympathetic to money and employment vibrations!

Once you are sitting in front of your prospective employer, send a beam of loving light straight from your heart into theirs. This helps to open the channels of communication. Remember that you are two ordinary human beings, no greater or lesser than each other. Relax and enjoy the interview. If this job is for your highest purpose, it will unquestionably become yours. If not, there is something far better out there. You just need to open up to the possibility. Whatever the outcome, remember to light a candle of thanks to the Universal consciousness for its help. The gods deserve acknowledgement.

How to Enhance a Business Venture

If you really want to find out the most auspicious day to open your business, you need to consult a recognized astrologer. The placement of the planets can have a profound effect on how your business will progress over the years. Always make sure that Mercury's motion is direct, not retrograde. Make a special prosperity amulet that you can hang over the door. And consult a Feng Shui expert, or at least buy a good book on the matter, especially if you are planning to open an office, store, or restaurant. Balancing the energy of your workplace is of paramount importance in ensuring harmony, success, and longevity.

> The placement of the planets can have a profound effect on how your business will progress over the years

Take time to plant window boxes or to grow a special plant that you can put in the prosperity (north-west) corner of your work area. You should always put your money tills in this area, as it will automatically draw in further abundance. Look after your plants as you would your business. they live and breathe, just as your business lives and breathes. Lastly, light a candle on each full moon to thank the Universe for its continuing support.

Creating Miracles

Before we enter into the modus operandi of miracle-making, let's take a look at the meaning behind the word "miracle." It derives from the Latin *mirari*, meaning to wonder, which in turn derives from the Sanskrit *smaya* to wonder, the root of which is *smi*, meaning to smile! So there you have it: to create a miracle all you have to do is smile. But the world we create is often far from joyous and stops us from expressing that wonderful creative spontaneity that is ours by divine right. Our emotional make-up plays a vital role in how we respond or react to life, and it is through learning to take control of our feelings, rather than letting them run amok, that we begin to create a positive and loving attitude toward ourselves and toward all that we draw to us. To create miracles in our lives, we first need to re-educate ourselves in how to express our emotions safely. To do that we need to be in possession of a few more facts.

Notions and Emotions

Man is the shuttle, to whose winding quest
and passage through these looms
God order'd motions, but ordain'd no rest.

Henry Vaughan, 1622–1695

The word "emotion" is derived from the Latin *emovere* meaning to move. According to Latin grammar an "e" placed before a consonant means "to emit" – to send forth. Therefore the literal translation of the word "emotion" is to "emit motion." And to be e-motion-less means exactly that – not to be in motion; to be blocked.

We are all inherently born with five natural instincts: fear, anger, jealousy or zeal, grief, and love. When we allow ourselves to emit these in a healthy and positive way, we are wreathed in smiles from dawn to dusk. However, if these instincts become blocked through various forms of trauma, our feelings become distorted to such a degree that a completely different set of emotional hybrids replaces them. These hybrids thrive on negative thought, so how can we begin to spot a miracle – let alone manifest one – when a destructive emotional monster is voraciously consuming our minds? Remember: how we think is how we are.

We are all inherently born with five natural instincts: fear, anger, jealousy or zeal, grief, and love

The natural emotion of fear: This is our survival alarm bell, our physical protector. It allows us to respond instinctively to threatening situations and is the sixth sense that warns us when danger may be lurking.

The fear hybrid: Ever heard of the expression "frozen in fear"? This is expressed by blind panic and panic attacks, constant anxiety about what tomorrow may bring, any type of phobia (from spiders to high buildings), and feeling threatened by people and situations that may move or change. Often it takes a crash or a "disaster" of some kind to jolt us out of this frozen state so that we can begin to heal.

The natural emotion of anger: This allows us to assert ourselves with firmness; to put our foot down by saying "No" and meaning it! It shows us when we need to set new personal boundaries, due to the behavior of those around us becoming unacceptably invasive. It also helps us to identify the feeling of being trapped – "I can't stand this any more." Anger helps us to break out of restricted conditions that no longer serve us and spurs us on to greater heights.

The anger hybrid: This manifests itself as either violent physical or verbal eruptions of rage and hatred, or as festering pits of bitterness and resentment. It makes us blame others for allegedly "holding us back." And it creates intensely destructive self-hate. It can also render us sexually impotent, mentally powerless, and produce that destructive feeling of "Oh what"s the use – it's all so hopeless."

The natural emotion of jealousy or zeal: I prefer to use the word "zeal," because jealousy carries such negative connotations. This emotion encourages us to emulate that which we admire and revere. It literally drives us onto better ourselves by inciting healthy competition and ambition. It allows us to respect ourselves and take pride in who we are and what we do.

The jealousy hybrid: This shows itself as low self-worth, covered up by negative responses to anything and anyone.

It creates the mask-wearers – those who gossip behind the backs of others while being ultra-pleasant to their face, or who constantly ridicule other people's ideas and ambitions. It also produces continual competition through comparison, and is the emotional monster that the advertising industry has made its own.

> **When we allow ourselves to emit our five natural instincts in a healthy and positive way, we are wreathed in smiles from dawn to dusk**

The natural emotion of grief: Imagine what it would be like not to be able to cry, to be e-motion-less. This is a state from which many men suffer, due to "stiff upper lip" conditioning. Grief allows us to express our sadness healthily when our loved ones die, and to express what lies in our hearts when something touches us deeply. It also enables us to release blocked emotions, so that we can move forward in our relationships. There are two types of tears: crying for help, and wracking sobs, which release the whole body from its emotional and physical pain. Grief is a completely natural expression, which allows us to reach out to others in our vulnerability so that we can share ourselves in love.

The grief hybrid: This is a deeply depressed state of mind. We become guilt-ridden, remorseful, self-pitying, and regretful. Some people get caught up in the past, dragging it with them like a ball and chain; others escape into becoming workaholics. Many also become victims to the "shoulds" and "oughts" in life. Others become either martyrs to strange causes or absorbed in other people's problems.

The natural emotion of love: Love allows us to explore harmonious and nurturing relationships and to create

successful working environments. Love is creative, inspiring, compassionate, and non-judgemental. It gives us the power to stand up and be counted, to take pride in how we express ourselves as individuals, and to guide us unerringly toward our own truths. It enables us to express our full range of emotions and encourages us to connect with the divine source. Love constantly moves us forward to greater heights of spiritual, mental, emotional, and physical expression.

The love hybrid: This turns in on itself to produce obsessive behavior expressed through paranoid possessiveness and unrealistic expectations of ourselves and others. People devoid of self-love are demanding and selfish, and will do anything to avoid being left alone. This leads many of us to hop from one relationship straight into another because we are desperately searching outside ourselves for someone to mend the gaping wound within.

Hybrid emotions enslave us to a victim consciousness, which prevents us from becoming who we truly are. Healing our emotional traumas enables us to set ourselves free to enjoy the kind of life we all deserve. It opens our hearts to receive those magical intuitive feelings and coincidental meetings that make life so rich, rewarding, and miraculous.

The first step toward self-healing is to make the decision to jump off the wheel of victim consciousness; to abandon the "he said," "she said" syndrome, the life of "shoulds" and "oughts."

The second step is actually to jump.

The third step is to die rather than allow yourself to clamber back on that treadmill again.

Making the Decision to Jump

One of the most important results
you can bring into the world
is the you that you really want to be.

Robert Fitz, The Path of Least Resistance

Once you have made the decision to find out who you really are, radical changes have to take place, not all of them immediately appealing. Those who have their heads stuck in the sand can feel very threatened by change, so don't be surprised if a certain amount of negative pressure comes your way.

 On a Monday night, during the waxing moon, light two blue candles anointed with lavender and rosemary oils, which bring in the vibration of healing. You could also add a drop of bergamot for protection. Place the candles on your altar in the centre of your circle of stones.

Light your incense, then allow yourself to relax and open your mind and heart. On a piece of paper write down what you want to change in your life. Be brutally honest. Allow yourself to feel any emotional response that might arise. Do you feel held back by certain situations or relationships? Do you really like where you live, and what you do? Write down whatever response comes to mind.

Take your piece of paper and offer it to the candle saying the following incantation five times:

Great Healing Powers
Come directly to me
Help me to hear and help me to see
So I may at last fly truly free.
So mote it be.

As you watch your paper turn to ash in a heatproof dish, open your heart and call out to the Universe (or to your deity) for help to come, in whatever form is for your highest good. Remember that what "should" happen is not necessarily what your higher self has in mind. This is a time of learning to trust.

For the next five nights light a blue candle, allowing it to burn down completely, and for a few moments empower your call for help and guidance. Help often comes during sleep, so make sure you have a pen and paper beside your bed to write down your dreams on waking. If you don't understand them immediately, allow a few days to go by and then read them again.

Be prepared for help and direction to come in strange ways – synchronistic and coincidental meetings, for example; information from a book; hearing something on the radio that makes your heart jump. That's the magic at work!

Jumping off the Wheel

> The Cheyenne man is not a man until he
> follows his dream and finds his medicine

> *Cheyenne saying*

The key to testing our sincerity to jump off the wheel of victim consciousness is to be willing to come to terms with our past actions. We have to learn to forgive ourselves, and then we can begin to forgive others who have caused us pain and discomfort. Our enemies expose us by bringing to the surface all our dark negativity and hateful thoughts, which we try to

repress and deny. We cannot move forward until we embrace and release these destructive tendencies.

The first law of occult science is that "energy follows thought." Once we have grasped this concept and gained a clearer insight into ourselves, the Universe often arranges coincidental meetings with our old enemies, just to see how far we have come in our quest to let go.

If you have a particularly difficult relationship with someone whom you are unable to confront physically, for whatever reason, but feel that it is high time for forgiveness, I suggest performing a simple ritual that can help release those negative bonds.

On a Wednesday night, during the waning moon, light five blue candles anointed with lavender, rosemary, and sandalwood. Place them in the shape of the five-pointed pentagram on your altar. Light some incense and relax.

Close your eyes and call up in your mind's eye the person with whom you are experiencing difficulties. Imagine that you are putting your hand on their heart, and feel the energy start to flow between you. Ask that person why they have come into your life, and what the lessons are that you need to learn from them. It is remarkable how quickly unpleasant emotions turn into accepting, loving ones once you understand the role you have both played in each other's life. When you feel complete, allow the person to present you with a "gift." This may take the form of words, feelings, or an image. Thank the person and tell them firmly, yet lovingly, that you are unconditionally willing to release them to their highest potential. See them floating away from you, and enjoy waving them farewell!

Light a green candle for them, as a gesture of harmony, place it on your altar in the centre of the pentagram, and allow it to burn out completely. While it is burning, draw a hatchet and on

The Universe often arranges coincidental meetings with our old enemies, just to see how far we have come in our quest to let go

the blade write both your names. As you finish, say the following incantation three times:

> *Bury the hatchet one, two, three*
> *It is no longer of service to me*
> *The bond is broken*
> *So mote it be.*

You can either burn the drawing or bury it in the garden.

Performing rituals like this does make a miraculous difference. You will find that either the person drops safely out of your life, because they no longer have a role to play in your growth, or your attitude toward the relationship becomes much more compassionate and positive.

As we take responsibility for what we create, we become more aware of who we are and less afraid of being alone. The world takes on a new look and suddenly we can see a way forward.

The Magic of Synchronicity

God gave us being without cause.
Give it back again without cause.
Gambling yourself away is beyond any religion.

Rumi, 1207–1273

Our soul's desire is to expand and grow, so that we can raise ourselves to the height of our creative expression in a truly loving way. The Universe is constantly helping us to do this, by arranging miraculous happenings that point us in the right direction. Sadly, most of us are so embedded in our fear, or so preoccupied with trivial matters, that we disregard them or fail to take advantage of them, even when they stare us in the face. The most obvious miracles-in-the-making are coincidental or synchronistic meetings.

When you look back over your life, especially during moments of great change, you will undoubtedly find that certain people with key parts to play appeared in the strangest of circumstances to help you reshape your future. Once change is under way, these people (who may be friend or foe, depending on the type of experience you need in order to move forward) often disappear as quickly as they appear. Their task is done. These synchronistic experiences open up situations in which we need to remain, until we have overcome the set of karmic tests or lessons facing us. Once these are completed and we are ready and willing to move on, life opens up again, the Universe creates further meetings, new people come into our lives, and once again change and growth are on the way.

This is the true miraculous magic of life, constantly working for us, night and day. When the time is right and we are ready and, above all, willing to receive, messages from the Universe appear in all sorts of ways to inspire us and to light the path ahead – be it in fleeting moments with strangers, overheard conversations, through books and magazines, or through so-called disasters.

Disasters can be Positive!

And if you look at the lives of all the men and
women, the great achievers, you will see that each
without exception faced and transcended tribulation,
illness, bankruptcy, or failure before they reached
a pinnacle of human endeavor.

Stuart Wilde, The Force

Disasters come in a colourful array: physical injury, bankruptcy, illness, death, loss of a home, break-up of a relationship, and so on. Such crises literally bring our lives to a full stop. The only thing that remains is to take a good long look at ourselves, reassess our lives and attitudes, dust ourselves down, and start all over again.

Remarkable achievements have been made by people suffering appalling traumas and tragedy. Such disasters seem to release some sort of primal urge to survive, rebuild and do a whole lot better the next time. Disaster humbles us, and through humility we become more compassionate and understanding. Through illness and physical injury we can find the courage and inner strength that perhaps were

missing while we struggled on; through the death of a loved one we can explore our grief and question the fear of our own mortality. Such experiences catapult us into a depth of healing that clears the way for our souls to guide us back to the true path.

Disasters are nature's way of giving us a second chance. Sadly, most of us are so out of touch with who we are that these experiences are viewed in terror and despair, rather than as vital turning points. If we continue to ignore the warning signals that we need to change or alter course, we have only ourselves to blame. Help is available, if we have the courage to reach out, and who better to help than someone who has already been through the experience? We are all each other's students and teachers. Once a little time has passed, we can look back on uncomfortable experiences from a much more secure and forgiving place, heave a sign of relief – and smile!

Author's Note

People always say that writing a book changes your life. Well, believe me, it does! *The Wiccan Handbook* took root as an idea several years ago, when I was needing to make a change in my life. My aim was to move to the West Country. Instead I found myself on a plane to Mexico. This unexpected turn of events made me open my heart and mind to the call of that higher part of me that has always been my mentor and guide. It also gave me the opportunity to look back over my life to see how the next chapter of my destiny had revealed itself – but never a moment before I was ready.

I realized that, even in childhood, magic and those unseen forces were such a part of my psyche that I never questioned them. Later I lost my way, because I forgot about the magic. But it was always there, waiting to be embraced. Once I remembered it, life took on a different slant. Suddenly I discovered that every single step I took was another on the path toward harmonizing with my higher self – with the Universe, my guides, ancestors, and angels, who were walking beside me every step of the way. Books began to fall into my hands, wise people and teachers would appear at precisely the right moment to shunt me through yet another barrier, workshops would call me to attend. I found that I had no choice but to give up my job of work which, although lucrative, gave me no real satisfaction. I began to study: theology, Catholicism, spiritualism, herbalism, healing, feminism, cabbalist teachings, Mayan culture, Native American practices, Egyptology, numerology, astrology, and witchcraft. And for the first time I began to love my life.

My thirst for the truth is unquenchable, as is my search for the understanding of who we are. Rest assured, there have been moments when I've wanted to run away – it seems that the more you learn, the more exposed you become. But the only solution is to go right on. The one thing I take forward with me is a clear understanding that, when we open up to magic, simply anything can happen. Yet magic comes at its own pace and in its own time, depending on your own state of awareness. Nothing can happen until you are ready to receive it.

I hope that *The Wiccan Handbook* has given you a taste for the magic of witchcraft. The adventure is there. You just need to open your arms and say yes!

And watch out, there's magic about.

Index